Lady
LOST

The Story of the
HONEYMOON COTTAGE
in Jerome, Arizona

The Honeymoon Cottage, Jerome, AZ   HEILEBEN

MARGARET GRAZIANO

Lady LOST

THE STORY OF THE HONEYMOON COTTAGE
IN JEROME, ARIZONA

FIVE STAR PUBLICATIONS, INC.
CHANDLER, ARIZONA

www.JeromeLadyLost.com

Linda F. Radke, President
Five Star Publications, Inc.
POB 6698
Chandler, AZ 85246-6698
480-940-8182

Publisher's Cataloging-In-Publication Data

Library of Congress Cataloging-in-Publication Data

Black-Graziano, Marge.

Lady lost : the story of the Honeymoon Cottage in Jerome, AZ /
by Marge Black-Graziano. – 1st ed.

   p. cm.
ISBN-13: 978-1-58985-152-8
ISBN-10: 1-58985-152-8

1. Honeymoon Cottage (Jerome, Ariz.) 2. Historic buildings – Conservation
and restoration – Arizona – Jerome. 3. Jerome (Ariz.) – Buildings, structures,
etc. 4. Douglas, Lewis W. (Lewis Williams), 1894-1974 – Homes and haunts –
Arizona – Jerome. I. Title.
NA7238.J47B53 2009
690'.8370979157 – dc22

                    2009011221

Printed in the United States of America
PROJECT MANAGER: Sue DeFabis
COVER DESIGN BY: Kris Taft Miller
INTERIOR LAYOUT BY: Koren Publishing Services

Acknowledgements

*T*hanks to all the many people who helped bring the lady to where she is today. Each person contributed to the process of rebuilding. Some were only with the Lady for a short period of time and others were enjoined from the beginning to the end. Without all of them, nothing would have been accomplished. Each person has a special place in my heart and the heart of the Lady.

Harry Stewart – General Contractor, friend and long time resident of Jerome and restoration expert
Nancy and Tracy Wiesel – friends and owners – Raku Gallery – long time residents of Jerome
Sam Cole – Cole Brothers Tile – friend of Marge who visited the Honeymoon Cottage the first time with her
Dave Vogel – Townie and friend
Danny Rowley – Olde Town Electric – friend and electrician who re-wired the lady
Robert Rose – Townie and friend and plumber
Robert (Bo) Wilson – friend and painter of the Lady

Victor Senne – Tile setter who tiled the patio and front stairs
Walter Aker – Neighbor and friend and master wood worker who built new as original French doors and windows and shelving and so much more, and assistant to Harry Stewart.
Scotty Nesslerode – Townie, friend and gardener to the Lady
Donald Skimin – Finish carpenter
Michael – Helper to Harry and Walter
Darin Lewis – Townie, friend and dry stack wall builder, and helper to Harry and Walter
Zack Druen – Stucco and helper to Harry and Walter
Blue Boelter – townie and architect for the Little House
Eric Morice – Platinum Paint Company Owner - painter
Scott McMillian – Wood floor specialist
Phil Wright – General Contract
Richard Peek – Roofer
Dennis Woodman – Townie and friend and wood worker who built the scrren doors to look and act as originals
A big thank you to anyone who helped in the restoration of the Lady who I have missed.

A big thanks to Linda Radke of Five Star Publications, who made the journey with me from a bunch of local newspaper monthly articles to a real book. Also, to Jennifer Christensen, the editor who suffered along with me as I struggled to put it all together in book form.

To all the folks who sat and read with me, again and again, to make sure everything made sense.

Mostly, to the Lady for offering me the opportunity to experience and tell the story of the Honeymoon Cottage.

Prologue

*O*nce upon a time there was a charming young lady who carried herself quite well. She came from a very good family that wanted only the best for her. Raised in wealth, nurtured in what some would feel was extreme excess, her background was bred from reckless adventure and risk-taking with the lure of great riches as a reward. Conceived in 1920 and completed in 1921, her domain as a youngster was to overlook the entire Verde Valley in Arizona. She grew up amidst rough and tumble folks who were not always the best mannered, yet she always presented herself as nothing less than elegant. From her copper patina top to her base surrounded by flowers and shrubs, she was always perfect.

Loved and admired by all, many happy times surrounded her as she matured into a young woman. As she grew older, times changed, and people began to care about her less and less. Neglected and abused, she was stripped of her adornments and left bare and empty. Longing for past times of gaiety, joy and happiness, dreaming of yesteryear and the sense of belonging she once enjoyed, she reminisced about the importance of having people care for you. Forgotten and lost, falling into a state of apathy and depression, her head was no longer *held high. Shoulders sagging, her very foundation shifted and settled. Her appointments were tarnished or stolen, and she languished in neglect. Losing the very luster and dignity that once set her above all her peers, an old, abused woman was left standing in place of the young, luminous lady she once was.*

A few times over the years someone would flirt with her and pretend to love her. Smiling and enjoying what seemed to be a restoration to her old self, she would be severely disappointed to find it was only a sham. Deeper and deeper into despair she fell, sleeping a lot more now, lost in reverie of a better time gone by. Years slid by, one after another, and nothing mattered anymore. All she had was long gone, and her beauty faded and dulled as she slowly passed into obscurity.

Then a soft voice began whispering kind words, causing her to awaken slightly. Listening as loving comments were made about her old self, she thought, "Someone understands me! Someone is looking into my heart and sees my inner self and what I once was and what I can be again. Someone will love me and care about me." She sighed, smiled and knew that in the near future she would once again shine as the jewel she was in her youth.

Eighty years after her birth, the Honeymoon Cottage was purchased by Marge Graziano, and a wonderful journey – that continues to this day, began.

This analogy is about the Lewis W. Douglas home, also known as the Honeymoon Cottage. This home is a National Historic Landmark and is listed on the National Historic Register. The home was built in 1921 in Jerome, Arizona, by James (Jimmy "Rawhide") Douglas as a wedding gift for his son and daughter-in-law, Peggy. The couple lived in the home for just over a year before moving to New York City. Although they returned several times on business, they never again lived in Jerome. Over the years, the home had been neglected, abused and pseudo-remodeled, and needed repairs were either done badly or simply covered up. Any dignity the Lady enjoyed was torn asunder, much as her lovely deck was demolished and her stately columns thrown over the wall at her borders and down the hill.

Today the Lady stands tall once more overlooking her beloved Verde Valley. Her stately columns again support a deck complete with the original wrought iron rails. She is enjoying a complete makeover after a total tear out, right down to her plaster and lathe. She looks forward to her new dress and her rightful position again as the Jewel of Jerome.

Marge Graziano obtained the Honeymoon Cottage in October 2001 and began restoration in November of the same year with the assistance of the finest craftsmen in Jerome. Harry Stewart, the general contractor, along with a host of dedicated sub-contractors and workers, attended to the Lady's every whim. Their desire to restore her to her former glory gave rise to an interesting journey indeed.

Dry stack walls are again exposed, as 80 years of debris have been removed. Too many rusty cans to count; old wood-shingle roofing; hundreds of glass bottles and broken crockery; and an assortment of toys, kitchen items, no longer useable appliances and odds and ends were all found "over the hill," including the original iron railings for the parapet walls on the deck. Tons of fill dirt leveled the yard. Topsoil preceded the grass sod, and hundreds of shrubs, bushes and plants now grace her borders. Dressed in yellow and blue, with new shutters framing her windows and a new architectural shingle blue roof, the Lady once again shares herself with guests and visitors. She stands proudly today as she did in 1921 when she was gifted to a favorite son and his wife. She looks forward to the future and her legacy as the Jewel of Jerome.

In March of 2001, I was invited to a gathering in Sedona, Arizona. This meeting of insurance agents from a three-state area brought many old friends together. Having a free afternoon mid-week led me to take a trip to Jerome, the "old sliding-down-the-hill town." I remembered stories and legends from long ago visits to the "Hippie Town on the Hill". It turned out that this was the beginning of an unexpected adventure that changed my life in ways I never could have imagined.

I hadn't been to Jerome for many years and had only memories of an old town on a mountainside with dilapidated houses – many reduced to nothing but their foundations – and a ribbon of odds-and-ends businesses that wound along a couple of streets. That March day was warm, and as I wandered in and out of the many new and upgraded shops, I was surprised to see how much Jerome had changed. The town itself seemed abuzz with new energy and renewed life. Where years ago buildings in need of repair once stood deserted, there were now new building fronts, shiny glass windows and upscale merchandise for sale.

Wednesdays in Jerome are quiet, and as I made my way in and out of various shops, I stopped in a gallery called Raku. As I walked in, my eyes were drawn to a large marble horse head sculpture in the corner by the window. The marble carving swiveled on a pin set on a granite base. The cost put me off, and I left the shop after a few minutes.

As I returned to the street and later at the resort in Sedona and for weeks afterward, the horse head kept finding its way into my thoughts. The business card from the gallery that I had placed in my wallet kept slipping out as I reached for cash. Feeling a strange pull from the horse head, I dialed the shop several times to see if the sculpture was still there only to hang up before the phone actually rang. The price was so high, yet I was trying to convince myself that I needed to have the sculpture.

In July, a friend and I drove to Jerome to spend the

night at the supposedly haunted Grand, a former hospital and now a wonderful historic hotel. After we settled in, we walked into town. Sam, like myself, had not been to Jerome for many years, and it was a walk of rediscovery for him as it had been for me months earlier. As we walked around the corner past the Warehouse, a restored private residence and the oldest surviving building in the town, we saw a gentleman loading wood into a pickup truck. We asked him if he lived in Jerome and if he could tell us anything about the homes in the town and what was happening with all of the property restorations. This casual encounter evolved into a lengthy conversation and one of my first friendships in Jerome. During our time together, Dave gave us a tour of his own home (just a few houses down the street from the Warehouse) and told us that he and his wife were in the process of restoring it.

As we continued on down the winding streets into town, we passed the Raku Gallery. I wondered if the horse head was still there. Of course it was. This day Nancy Weisel, the shop owner, was working. I admired the horse head again but was still struggling to justify the cost. As we spoke with Nancy about what we were doing in town, we looked out over the Verde Valley through the gallery's floor-to-ceiling windows. Sam pointed to a house just below the historic Little Daisy Hotel, now also a restored private home. It turned out that Nancy knew quite a bit about the home. The house sat at the end of a road surrounded by many trees, and it looked very secluded. We were intrigued. Could we drive down to see the house?

Winding our way down Douglas Road then through the chain-link fence entrance past the deserted old mine building, now storing ore samples, we approached the large yellow house. Nancy told us that the home was built by James Douglas, the owner of the Little Daisy Mine, for his son, Lewis. The home was a wedding gift for Lewis and his wife Peggy; it was their Honeymoon Cottage. Lewis and Peggy lived in the house for only a short time. After that, the house had a succession of owners, many of them never actually living in the home. Renters and periods of vacancy had taken quite a toll on the property. As we walked around the outside, I had the strangest feeling that I was walking the grounds of *my* home. There were areas where it was evident that the house had been neglected and poorly maintained, however, I was only seeing what it could be and not what it was.

At this point, we had not even made it inside the house. This was one of those times when you have a gut feeling and you just know that you have to follow it. We went back to the Raku Gallery to speak more with Nancy. She could probably get us the keys to go inside. We said we would stop by on Sunday before we headed back to the Phoenix-metro area and let her know about the sculpture.

However, when Sunday came, the time got away from us, and we did not see Nancy. The horse head and the house were going round and round in my head, and on Sunday evening I called Nancy at home. She was coming to the Valley on Monday to catch a flight from Sky Harbor Airport and said she could deliver the sculpture to my home: I could live with it for a week, and if I didn't like it, she would pick it up on her way back to Jerome. She also said she knew how we could get the keys to the Honeymoon Cottage.

The following weekend, another trip to Jerome afforded us entry to the house. The warmth and aura of the house enveloped us immediately. When things are as they are supposed to be, all the little pieces fall into place, just like putting a puzzle together. Little did I know what a challenging puzzle the house would become. On October 8, 2001, ownership of the Honeymoon Cottage was transferred from

Don Hopkins to me, Margaret Graziano, and the greatest journey of my lifetime began.

I knew I was in for a major restoration project. I began by searching for someone who knew old houses in Jerome and was willing to handle this scarred beauty with care and tenderness. I vowed not to rip into her with no regard for her feelings as so many others had done before. I found one contractor, a Jerome resident named Harry Stewart, who told me he was just too busy to take on another job. I liked Harry immediately. Though he said he would not be available for quite a while, as he had several other jobs stacked before mine, I knew Harry was the right man for the task, and I was willing to wait until he was available.

Harry has lived in Jerome for many years and has experience with many other historical town restorations. He knows old houses. We spoke about what needed to be done and how very difficult it was going to be. By then, I had started to think of the Honeymoon Cottage as a living, breathing person, complete with its own personality and character. As I stood with Harry on the front lawn looking at the house, I heard her calling to me across the years, a timeless echo: "Find me," she whispered through the ages. "I'm still here. Understand me. Look into my heart and see my inner self. Learn what I once was and envision what I can again become. Love me and care about me." How very quickly her spirit had fused itself with mine.

Never in my wildest dreams would I have predicted the events that ensued over the next two years. What has happened to me, the people around me and the town where the house was built could not have been foreseen. Travel along with me through the renovation of the Lewis W. Douglas Honeymoon Cottage as seen through the eyes of the Lady, the Jewel of Jerome. I hope that as you read the journal I have kept for the past few years, you, too, will feel the magic and the mystery the Lady exudes upon everyone she chooses to wrap her arms around and make a part of her world.

The Lewis W. Douglas
Honeymoon Cottage

In 1921, James Douglas, the owner of the Little Daisy Mine, once the largest copper producing mine in the world, gave his son Lewis a wedding gift – a wonderful house with a picturesque view of the Verde Valley. The home of the newly married couple became known throughout the region as the Honeymoon Cottage, though almost from the moment we met, I've known the house as "The Lady."

The young couple lived in Jerome for just a year before leaving the Lady. Lewis enjoyed an enviable career throughout his lifetime, traveling the world in splendor as the Lady slowly slid into obscurity through neglect, abandonment and mistreatment. Eighty years later, a journey began to restore her original birthright.

*   *   *

In November 2001, a young woman walked around a newly purchased house with her mother. With uncanny vision and certainty, the young girl announced, "I am going to get married here!" With no suitor waiting in the wings, Mom just smiled at her daughter's comment. But the Lady knew better. Sure enough, a few months later Carrie had a ring on her finger. Little did we know then that this was just the beginning. The Lady still had a few more tricks up her sleeve. As the months passed during her restoration, she pulled out a few of these tricks – a vineyard in Wilcox, a tasting room in Jerome and a wedding planner with her own wedding creating the blueprint for the future.

Around Thanksgiving I received an unexpected phone call from Harry. He wanted to know if I was still interested in having him work on the house. The building permit for his present job was not yet approved, and the work had to be postponed. This was the first of many strange and special occurrences still to come. Through the ensuing months, as Harry and his company worked to restore the home, wonderful friendships were formed, support from the community overflowed, and unusual events took place. I acquired a special identity in a very special town that gave me the opportunity to make a difference in the lives of others, and it was all thanks to the Lady.

In December 2001, total restoration began that included new wiring; copper plumbing; the installation of a new boiler and water heater; raising a settled section of the dining room; new wall finish; fresh paint; stripped, sanded and refinished original Douglas fir floors; repaired windows; some new windows; stainless steel window cranks, manufactured to look like the originals; stripped and polished old nickel hinges; and drawer pulls. Following the original plans, an entire pillared deck was restored and rebuilt. An architectural blue shingle roof topped off the house, as well as too many numerous other things to mention.

Tons of fill dirt leveled the yard, topsoil preceding new sod, and hundreds of shrubs, bushes and plants now grace her borders. Dressed in yellow and blue with new shutters framing her windows, the Lady happily shared herself with guests at the joining of Jason Francisco Miller and Carrie Janell McLoughlin Black in marriage, the first of many happy occasions to be celebrated with her blessing. The Lady smiles today as she looks forward to the future and her rekindled legacy as the Jewel of Jerome.

However, I am getting ahead of myself. Let us go back to the beginning of the journey and how we arrived at this special wedding day.

Working Undercover

A look at the exterior of the house will reveal nothing of what is hidden beneath. The Lady is like a great Southern belle in a hoop dress, with yards and yards of crinoline supporting her cascading skirts.

The cracks in the stucco that appear small and inconsequential belie the extent of the damage to the structure. Over the years, the cracks have been sloppily covered over with heavy paint until they became too large to hide. The paint just slides into the cracks, while the openings remain. The damage underneath the cracked stucco has not yet revealed itself, and one can only guess what remains hidden.

Some problems we encountered immediately included carpet laid over wood flooring; new tile layered over the old; French doors nailed shut; windows unable to open due to missing cranks; and a slow water leak in the basement dismissed as overflow from the hot water heater. When it rains, runoff across an uneven cement driveway along the west side of the house allows water to flow freely into the old coal room in the basement. A roof that is no more than rotten plywood sags over the patio where the deck once stood.

The Lady groans beneath years of neglect, the weight of what she must bear in restoration heavy on her spirit.

I begin in the basement. The old coal burning boiler, the size of a small vehicle, must be taken apart and removed. It was assembled with individual cast iron sleeves that fit one into the other, allowing the boiler to be built as large as needed. Extracting it from the basement became a major challenge as the poured cement walls were built around the assembled boiler. The stairs leading out of the basement are narrow and steep, and the old boiler weighs as much as a herd of elephants. (It may be just that hard to move.) Working a day and a half, Harry Stewart, our general contractor, and his assistants dismantle the old beast section by section and carry it out, stacking it in pieces near the back of the garage. What to do with this bygone monster will be decided at another time. The hot water heater is leaking and must be replaced. The small gas boiler that took the place of the coal burner years ago must also be replaced. How easy it would have been to take care of these problems as they arose instead of just covering them up or doing makeshift repairs. What a needless affront to the Lady's sensibilities.

The many water pipes in the basement are rerouted and attached high against the north basement wall. The collection basin that used to hold a sump pump and that was filled with leaking water will be filled in with cement to create a level surface that will hold a washer, dryer and laundry tub. The two old refrigerators that have been stored next to the basin must find another home, which may be the dump. The cement driveway will be broken up, the ground leveled and new cement laid to channel the water away from the house. The old coal chute, now covered with a piece of cardboard, a black plastic bag and a layer of cement that leaks with every rain, will be fixed. The water would stand for weeks in the coal room, creating a musty smell and presenting a health and safety concern. The Lady can now breathe a sigh of relief.

One week later, the house surprises and delights me. In the dining room, the crew pulls up roll upon roll of deteriorating carpet. The kitchen floor, now free of its timeworn layers of old asbestos, stick-down tiles and sheet goods, finally lays naked and bare, revealing lovely unfinished Douglas fir tongue-and-groove flooring. The living room floor is painted brown, concealing the same wonderful tongue-in-groove wood.

The laundry room, formerly a screened-in cooling and mud room, reveals a badly deteriorated section of flooring under a plywood sheet that will have to be replaced. However, this disappointment is offset by the discovery of a secret no one expected the Lady to reveal – a small root cellar! Cream, milk, eggs, vegetables and other food items were stored there to keep them from spoiling. How long the small root cellar went hidden and unknown one can only guess. I slide sideways between the dryer and the old wooden icebox and peer down into the opening – a dark and forbidding cavern of pitch black.

The small back bedroom carpet is easily pulled up, and the wood underneath proves to be in good condition. Unfortunately, the small bathroom is another story. A claw-foot tub once occupied part of the bathroom next to a wall where a despicable fiberglass shower that has splashed water onto the carpet in competition with the overflowing toilet now stands. The rotted ceiling in the basement is ample evidence that their match had gotten out of control. The results are a destroyed bathroom floor and a ruined basement ceiling, an issue I will deal with later.

The front entry powder room provides another glimpse into the Lady's neglect. A lovely ivy vine grows up the southern side of the house, climbing up toward the second floor master bedroom. This vine provides a home to a multitude of small birds and insects, and the contrast of its dark green color is striking against the light yellow of the house. The vine grows rapidly, seeking any foothold it can find in its upward journey. One small stem finds an opening in the stucco and brick. It meanders persistently in its walled prison, trapped between the inner and outer walls with just enough light to live, moisture from its parent plant and no way to escape its cell. Harry tells me of this latest discovery, and we laugh over the thought that we could have an indoor greenhouse with no effort at all.

This handful of minor setbacks is quickly forgotten in my joy at finding most of the wood flooring in an excellent and very workable condition. The wood is warm and inviting, begging to be refinished. Two doorways in the kitchen and butler's pantry hint of long lost swinging doors, their past existence evident by brass plates at the door jams. I have a choice: reinstall swinging doors or replace the areas where the brass plates are with wood.

Two Weeks Later

*T*he weather is cooler and jackets are necessary now as I drive up to Jerome and see the leftover snow clinging to the crevices of the hillsides. The front door screen has been removed, having been torn open by the wind several weeks ago, its closing mechanism now broken. This is the same wind that must have blown open the dining room French doors in the middle of the night.

The house is cold as I enter. Most of the radiators were removed when the carpet and flooring were stripped. I see the large cracks at the outer edges of the dining room and wonder why this problem was covered up instead of being addressed. It is like trying to hide a wrinkle with a lot of makeup. The Lady must have cringed when a 1947 newspaper was rolled up and pushed into the cracks of her walls. (Harry was the one to discover this atrocity.) "Hiding the problem isn't going to solve it," she must have thought as the paper slowed the draft flowing through the fissure. Drywall placed over the original lathe and plaster once masked the shoddy repair, but now, many years later, the walls exhibit a spotty black mold where the rain seeped through the exterior cracks and sought escape. The water was captured by

17

the newspaper patch that held onto the moisture, fostering the growth of mildew and mold.

The original plaster walls, painted Douglas green, (a special shade of green paint that the mine owners used to paint most of their buildings), and a few other colors, hid behind the drywall. The original light fixtures were long gone and plated over. (Harry and Danny would later find live wires wrapped in silk behind these painted plates.) Inexpensive brass-plated fixtures were installed to provide lighting. A dining room chandelier hanging in the entryway was so low that a tall man could easily crack his head on it. "Oh, the indignity of it all," the Lady sighed. "I have been reduced to a cheap imitation of my former stately self."

As Harry continues to remove the drywall, the large cracks in the brick walls show how this section of the house has settled. Most of the settling happened either as the house was being built or soon after completion. The home, like most others in Jerome, was built on bedrock and fill dirt.,What little vegetation grew in the area where the smelter was, was planted close to the house. Watering of the bushes and flowers provided moisture, and the soft wet ground easily allowed the dining room section of the house to settle.

A large picture window with the drywall now gone shows the frame to be anything but original. It appears that it was originally two small-paned windows on each side of a large plate glass window. Pulling back wooden frames reveals the original marking left behind when it was covered up. Some areas of the original plaster have buckled, victims of gravity and time. Gravity takes a toll on everything, though not uniformly. There are areas where the lathe and plaster still appear new and other areas where creativity will have to be employed to solve the problem of "sag and drag." Harry will have to use mesh to hold some of the areas together to preserve the integrity of the wall. Sounds a bit like a girdle, perhaps, but a Lady must be held together to be well dressed.

Harry and Walter Aker (a neighbor who is working with Harry) are meticulous, careful and clean. Their hands are gentle and loving as they kindly undress the Lady. She shares willingly with them her most hidden secrets knowing that she'll soon be re-clothed.

Drywall coming off ceilings and walls reveals original plaster beneath. The back of the house dropped, settled and cracked as brick and stucco hung on, grasping at a structure that will soon collapse. Harry and Walter will shore it up, pour a new cement foundation underneath and bring the separated edges together again. Harry's plans include tying into the sagging part of the cottage with giant come-a-longs and pulling it back to be supported and held by the main, stable body of the house. Once this is accomplished, cracks will be repaired and the integrity of the walls restored. In time, the upstairs room, with its awkwardly slanted floor, will also be righted and leveled.

As the ceiling in the dining room is removed, old pack-rat nests are disturbed. They have been living comfortably here for a long time. "Seek another place, you rascals," the Lady whispers. "And take all your debris and rubble with you! You have been in my hair for far too long now."

I am anxious to move forward, but a death in his family means that Harry must put the job on hold for a week or so. The holidays come and go, and then Harry is back to the task. His love of old houses is matched only by mine, and I am confident that his expertise and skill coupled with my encouragement will bring the past to life and restore the Lady's beauty and dignity. Gentle, skillful hands pry away years of dirt and grime, animal nests and droppings, water damage and faulty repairs. Harry and Walter have caring hands that soothe wind and weather damage, defying past neglect and pulling the Lady to her feet. The Lady is embarrassed for me to see what has been hidden under her ragged clothing for so many years. At times, she is very subdued as Harry and I invade her most private places. The mystery she affords all of us enthralls me. In her acceptance of our invasion, we must move slowly and carefully and be gentle so as not to frighten her. The clues of her past are held tightly to her chest, and to tear haphazardly and recklessly into her bruised and battered soul would cause her to hide from us completely, never revealing the truth. We gently caress her with tender appeals, finally earning her trust. Step by step, her inner beauty is revealed, bringing forth new revelations.

The Lady's pulse quickens just a bit as she eavesdrops on our conversations. She is delighted as our talk turns to design plans and furnishings. The Lady smiles as we find her ribs and tickle them with brooms and brushes, sweeping away layers of old animal nests and debris. The winter sun warms her very bones, the exposed lathe in surprisingly excellent condition after all these years. She eagerly awaits a new face and grins at the prospect of now open (formerly nailed shut) French doors in the living room. She experiences a long lost feeling of hope for a future she never envisioned.

More Discoveries

$\mathcal{A}$s Harry, Walter, and Danny Rowley from Old Town Electric tackle the challenge of restoration, surprises lie in store for us all. The mystery deepens as to just how the Lady looked in her youth. The house's original architectural plans elude the search that Harry and I undertake, and some avenues lead to dead ends. But interest and concern outweigh discouragement, and old paths are re-traveled in the hope of finding new clues that will help solve the mystery of the Honeymoon Cottage.

This same weekend, a visit to the Douglas Mansion provides a new lead. John, the manager of the Jerome State Park, is generous with his advice and has been helpful with the restoration. "Call Ann at the Arizona Historical Museum in Tempe," he advises.

Throughout this early period of the renovation process, I continued my search for the original architectural plans. A trip to the Arizona Historical Society proved fruitless; conversations with local townsfolk led nowhere. Then I heard about the Jerome State Park having found the original plans for the Douglas Mansion, now the State Park. The Douglas Mansion was the home of James Douglas, the owner of the

Little Daisy Mine, the largest copper producing mine in the world at one time. The architects who drew up the plans for the Douglas Mansion were from the same firm that had drawn up the plans for the Little Daisy Hotel and, supposedly, the Honeymoon Cottage.

I had spoken with the Jerome Historical Society, a most helpful organization, and hit a dead end there as well. They did not have the plans and didn't know where to find them. In desperation, I contacted the Arizona Historical Society again, following John's suggestion, and this time I hit pay dirt, as they say. I spoke with a person who knew where the film was that had the plans for the Douglas Mansion. Maybe, just maybe, the plans for the Douglas home would be on that same 50 mm film. The same architects – Lescher, Kibbey & Mahoney, the Architectural Firm that drew up the plans for the James Douglas home also handled the Lewis Douglas home. The home was designed as French Country style in honor of George Clemenseau, the French Ambassador and friend to James Douglas.

I was so excited that I made a special trip into Tempe to the Historical Society. Luckily, this time I met up with a young man who, in exchange for a digital camera I had and didn't know how to use, promised he would seek out the film for me. He found the film, made me paper copies of the film (no one in Arizona has the projector necessary to show the film, which was made in Germany), and the Arizona Historical Society was now in possession of a much-needed digital camera. I gave the small paper copies of the film to Harry, and he had them blown up into a readable size, just as if they were the original drawings, even down to the blue paper.

The dining room floor has been completely removed, both the carpet and the wood. Harry and Walter can now shore everything up. The dirt under the floor is hard and solid, having had years to settle and pack down. We balance on long sturdy beams that are in remarkably good condition considering their age. The Lady worried when the old flooring was removed, as old Douglas fir, once very common, is now scarce. I make phone calls to salvaged wood suppliers, which lead me to companies in several states along the East Coast. Finally, I locate a company in Virginia that recycles old Douglas fir from old buildings that have been torn down and also from old growths of Douglas fir. The Lady smiles, relaxes and is confident that whatever she needs, I will find it somewhere, somehow! The wood flooring will be replaced with "new" old Douglas fir from Virginia after everything is tied up and anchored securely.

Walking around the house, the many projects taking place at the same time make me think of a well-oiled machine. Harry is like a conductor, his orchestra consisting of his workers, everyone playing a finely tuned instrument in the symphony of the Lady's renovation. Each player brings with him years of experience and, most importantly, a genuine love of his work. This love and gentleness is manifest in the quality of their workmanship and mirrored in the supportive way the workers toil alongside one another to put the Lady back together.

The new wood flooring has arrived, bringing with it a great need for an experienced craftsman. Scott McMillan, a flooring specialist from Prescott, gets right down to the base of the Lady to rebuild her footings. He will strip the master bedroom of the brown paint that covers the warm wood flooring. He will lay the new old Douglas fir wood from Virginia in the dining room and relay the original flooring from the dining room elsewhere in the house. Some will be placed in the bathrooms, where the many-times-wet wood has been removed and discarded. Some of the wood will go upstairs in the master bath, where the large cast iron apron tub has been sitting precariously on water-damaged wood. How this 350-pound tub has held on without falling through the rotted flooring all the way down to the basement is a miracle. Harry and the workers remove the tub from the master bath and set it in the master bedroom until Scott can get the new wood flooring put down.

Scott will also strip the landing at the head of the stairs and refinish that floor, which is currently painted a stifling brown. He will ultimately oil, refinish and seal all the flooring in the house.

On my next visit to the house, I am greeted by a new dining room floor and two of the newly redone bathrooms. The mud room, (formerly a screened in porch off the kitchen), also has a new wood floor, and the other floors will be refurbished in fast order. Already, the warmth and feel of splendid wood flooring is evident throughout the home.

The Lady stands erect again. Her saggy bottom, which had settled into the ground creating the cracks in the walls and the slanting floor in the nursery upstairs is hoisted up and tied into the joists. She throws back her shoulders and holds her head high. Harry, Walter and Michael (on leave from making movies in Hollywood) use come-alongs to tighten up the strapping that now reaches back into the Lady's very core. Two large beams stand firm at an angle to the east side of the house, meeting the dining room's outer wall. Each day they are pushed a little tighter against the wall. Large steel straps tie into each beam of the dining room ceiling, and they are welded onto large steel poles, one in each corner of the room. "Ouch," the Lady murmurs as the wall comes together. Soon, the cracks meet up with each other until only a sliver of an opening remains where once there was a huge gaping crack. "Oh, goodness," she sighs. "It has been hard hunching over for so many years. I found it difficult to raise my head to see the sun rise with my back so bent. It is easier to breathe when I can stand upright, and my neck isn't crooked with pain any longer."

As the cement is poured under the walls and flooring of the dining room to create a new foundation, the Lady blushes with embarrassment that someone has peered under her petticoat. As the foundation dries and hardens, the Lady stands upright again, her embarrassment fading into calm pleasure at her newly corrected posture.

The bright light causes the Lady to blink as the morning sun beams into the living room through the old glass panes in the now-open French doors. The old rotted patio cover has been torn down. Although it was weather – and water-damaged wood, it did provide a small amount of shade. Now there is just the bright, wonderful sunshine. The original metal railings that fit between the parapet walls of the original deck were found below the house, down the hill, strewn over the second terrace where they were discarded many years ago. They laid under roofing material, grass cuttings and who knows what else for probably ten or more years. The fact that they aren't rusted and ruined is a testament to their quality. They are made of heavy steel and will be fitted back into their rightful place on the deck. Squinting into the sun, the Lady hopes the deck will soon be rebuilt. "Ladies of my time, you know, did not expose their fair skin to the sun."

Tearing off the old drywall that covered so many problems, we are surprised to find boards marked with the signatures of the men who originally built the house. Underneath the dining room floor and behind the studs and lathe are names and cities written in pencil on 1×4 boards. Sometime ago, I read somewhere that "every job you do carries your signature; sign your work with excellence!" The original builders must have taken this to heart.

As the ceilings come down, there are more interesting

surprises. In the living room, a mummified rat sits with arched back and tail wound around himself. At first glance, he appears alive, though in reality, he has been hidden for many years in his petrified state in the space between the first floor ceiling and the second floor. The old fiberglass insulation is removed from the outer walls, revealing evidence of many critters having lived at one time or another in the Lady's deep pockets.

Much of the old insulation has been wet at some time and is in need of replacement. The fiberglass is "nasty stuff," and Harry has trouble subcontracting with anyone willing to pull it out of the house. He and Walter end up doing it themselves, suffering the itching and discomfort that go along with such painstaking work. The plans are to clean it all out and then have new insulation blown in.

Harry climbs into the inner reaches of the house, up under the Lady's hat, and finds other fascinating animals. A live bat colony found a wonderful home in the topmost part of the closed off attic. The attic was always warm, even in cold weather, and stuffy and moist in the summer. The Lady inhales deeply as Harry opens up the closed venting, allowing fresh spring air to flow through. "Thank you," she breathes. "That old corset was so tight that I couldn't speak above a whisper." She exhales and clears her lungs of dust and debris. As the pollen of flowers and spring blooming trees floats into her now open airways, she revels in the sweet scent of nature. "For oh so long, I have felt as if I have been holding my breath. It is good to smell fresh air again."

Old nests from generations of feathered friends are swept out. Bat guano, insect homes and odd collections of "things" have been deposited in the attic. An old paperback romance novel; a metal tobacco tin with Prince Albert pictured on the front; an old steel can of Budweiser beer are but a few of the treasures found. If only these walls could talk. "We will piece together their stories," the Lady whispers in our ears.

Harry continues exploring and cleaning out the attic, and another discovery is made. The bookcase on the second floor landing was actually meant as a linen closet, and we have all been struggling to figure out what kind of doors it originally had. Harry finds the original closet doors to this "bookcase" in the far northern end of the attic under layers of insulation. He will reattach the doors and convert what has been used as a bookcase back to a linen closet. These small discoveries bring great joy to our team that is trying desperately to recreate the Lady without a set of plans from which to work.

The kitchen stands bare with just the bones of the Lady exposed. The "mud room" comes together as a newly designed breakfast room. A utility closet that was in the mud room is closed over. Cut out of the wall behind is the same space that now provides a niche for a chair and lamp, where one can sit and relax with a good book. This small room was where the maid lived. The root cellar will remain in this new kitchen eating area and will possibly even be used. When the Lady was young, the first family she housed ate each meal together in the formal dining room, but life today dictates a smaller, more intimate setting for breakfast.

Walter works on the door leading outside to the garden area and replaces the aluminum windows and inappropriate door that were placed there by someone in the past. Having a master wood worker as part of the crew is a definite advantage. Walter builds new windows and a door that look exactly as the originals. These windows in the breakfast room match the other multi-paned windows in the rest of the house. The view from the dinette area will be framed by a grape arbor, rose bushes and an herb garden.

The Lady giggles in anticipation and can hardly wait to see her garden flourish.

Walls are all stripped down to the lathe. Old plaster, with its distinctive "Douglas green paint," was mostly beyond repair and has been completely removed. Looking through the lathe to the outer layer of the Lady's thick brick walls shows the strength and character of her body. This is the cloak that holds the heat in the winter and keeps her cool in the summer. I marvel at the Lady's solid construction and think of the many hands that lay brick after brick to complete her. Modest, she turns her face away from the many eyes that view her nakedness. She knows that she must get through this assault on her privacy and that she will soon be clothed again in her finest garments.

High on the wall in the kitchen entryway is a bell box. The bells once alerted the servants to the room from which the residents were calling. They will be reconnected: a bell with a distinctive tone for each room. A front doorbell wire has been located, and new chimes have been ordered. The butler's pantry will have a swinging door leading into the formal dining room. This door will be ornamented, as a safety issue, with a small beveled glass window taken from the old front entry door. Walter will build a new front door to create a more impressive entry.

In the basement, flooring has been laid in the laundry room. The large squares of slate on the dry and level floor seem almost too pretty to be hidden under the Lady's skirts. Water pipes, now fewer in number, are straight, and the water hook-ups are ready for the washer, dryer and laundry tub. Shelving will be hung on the walls to store all the paint, solvents, tools, etc., that are a part of every homeowner's basement. "My undergarments have never been so pretty. My new boiler keeps my body warm in the winter, and my new 75-gallon water heater with re-circulating pump will mean there is no waste of water," the Lady thinks to herself. As all the water systems are checked, the Lady is pleased to discover her elimination system is in good working order. All the lead and asbestos-covered pipes have been replaced with copper, and water now flows through her veins as it should.

We bid the Lady goodbye and lock the door. I turn my head just a bit, as I believe I hear someone softly singing a song. I am not sure of the words or the melody, but I know that the music is flowing from the Lady's happy heart. Her joy is contagious, and we all feel the excitement. Everything that is dirty, dusty, rusty and nasty is gone. The old has been removed or repaired, and the new patiently awaits installation. Columns lay on the lawn awaiting a time when they will support the new deck. Radiators stand in rows like short little soldiers listening for the call to battle. They are ready to march into the house and take their rightful places, warming the Lady through winter's long chill. Cracked, broken cement on the driveway and the patio lie in hope that Harry will soon demolish them and give them a proper burial in the dump. A new generation of cement will then be poured, and a steppingstone path constructed that will encircle the Lady, meandering through an orchard and ornamental garden.

Heirloom irises from another era poke their thin leaves up through the debris on the hillside behind the house and reach for the sun. One wonders what color they will be. Now that the tear-down is complete, our patience is tested as the Lady is redressed in her finery. As spring approaches, her rebirth begins, much as the earth itself is renewed year after year after winter melts into spring.

Jerome... Mines, Men and Money – How it all Began

*L*ife in Jerome is hard rock, hard work, hard liquor and hard play, according to Jim W. Brewer, Jr. I will add "hard to get to!" says the Lady. Perched on a hill, Jerome in the early part of the eighteenth century was not easily accessible. There were no "real" roads, and horses, mules and burros were the transportation of the day. The scrappy early miners had diggings that grew into one of the greatest copper-producing mines in the world. From early inhabitants who prized the colorful stone of the mountain to the Spanish gold hunters, and then from General George Crook's pioneering scouts to Dr. James A. Douglas, grandfather of Lewis W. Douglas, they all saw potential in Jerome. With their own blood, sweat and tears, they chiseled a livelihood out of the mountainside, taming the wilderness in the process.

When the early settlers began blasting mines in search of mineral riches, there were 9,708,923 tons of ore averaging 3.47 percent copper, 2.07 ounces of silver and .07 ounces of gold to the ton. It all lay under 15,977,801 cubic yards of over burden. To obtain access to all these minerals, open-pit mining would have to begin. A new smelter was put in place to separate the ore from its residual compounds, and a suitable operation was established in Clarkdale, a small town built by William Clark, owner of UVX, (United Verde Exploration), for his workers and their families. This small town had all the latest modern innovations, underground utilities being but one of them. The new smelter provided room for expansion and facilitated the development of housing for the miners and their families. By 1929, the population of Jerome had swelled to 15,000. More copper was coming out of Arizona, through the labor of 2,345 miners than from any other state, and the United Verde Mine produced $29 million in ore in one year.

Then the Great Depression hit. In 1932, the price of copper had dropped to a level that could not sustain the mine owners or the workers. Soon the mine closed, and the smelter fires were doused. In 1935, Phelps Dodge bought the abandoned mine for $20.8 million and resumed production shortly thereafter. In 1953, when Phoenix-area newspaper headlines read, "END COMES TO FAMED JEROME MINING CAMP," Phelps Dodge had successfully recouped its investment, netting millions upon millions of dollars.

On March 15, 1953, the Jerome Historical Society (JHS) was born. The inspiration for forming this organization and the Mine Museum came from the late Jimmy Brewer Jr., who was the curator of the Tuzigoot National Monument. When the big mine closed on January 30, 1953, he addressed the town council, saying, "I don't think you people realize what you have here. If you don't do something about it, all you will have left of your town is a pile of rubble." Jerome's slogan, America's Largest Ghost Town, was Brewer's idea and has attracted tourists for many years. (Source: Jerome Chronicle, Fall & Winter, 1973–1974; Minutes of Jerome Historical

Society, Sunday, March 15, 1953; Jerome Chronicle, Spring, 1980; History in the Making, Summer 2002.)

The JHS is dedicated to the preservation of Jerome as a town of vital historical significance to the Verde Valley, to Arizona and to the West. The first project of the JHS membership was to build a mining museum. Today, the former Fashion Salon has been given new life as the Jerome Mine Museum, a memorial to all the people and activities of Jerome's historic past. (Source: Document in museum update records of 1991.)

Looking over my shoulder, the Lady reads along with me as I learn about the history of the Jerome Historical Society. She now understands why she was left alone and unloved for so long. We continue to read the names of the many townspeople who cared enough to give their time and energy to keep the JHS vibrant for over 50 years. She knows Jerry Vojnic, Peggy Tovrea, John Armstrong, Marge Mitchell, Joan Evans, Erica Raspberry, Mimi Currier, Diane Rapaport, Sharon Watson, Richard Flagg, and especially Nancy Smith, Pam Ravenwood and Ron Roope, present archivist.

Nancy is a longtime resident and good friend of mine and has been helpful with information about life in Jerome. The Lady smiles, thinking that Nancy has been around so long she literally knows where all the bodies are buried! I remember and am thankful to both Nancy and Pam for all of their help, even with the typing of this story. Ron has been an endless source of information and guidance and is never too busy to answer questions or seek out a fact for us.

The history of Jerome is colorful and interesting, both happy and sad. It is a story of the ups and downs of a town once populated with all kinds of people. The Lady reads about Jerome and is proud to have been a part of its history. She hopes I will go to the library and bring home some books that will help her learn even more about the town in which she lives.

She wonders if I know how the raw ore was processed and how a smelter worked. There was good and bad that came from the smelter. She was there when the air was so filled with sulfur that all the vegetation in Jerome died and nothing could grow in the dirty, smelly air that let little sunlight shine through.

Just What is a Smelter?

A smelter separates and purifies metal from raw ore. The steam shovels used to dig the Panama Canal all found a new home in Jerome. From the mine, ore goes to a crusher plant, a mechanized pestle-and-mortar apparatus of mammoth proportions. A great pounding bar gyrates inside a funnel-shaped mortar and crushes the ore, which empties out of the bottom. The ore is filtered by size, and a second crusher then reduces this filtered ore to pebble-sized bits and transports it to the concentrator plant. There, the ore is mixed with water and heavy oily reagents, then run through a revolving cylinder and agitated by compressed air. The minute metal particles cling to the resulting oil bubbles, and the sludge waste is carried off to a trailing pond. Then the copper-collecting bubbles are floated off and mixed with fluxing agents. This concentrate is fired and fed into a reverbera-tory furnace, in which the flame is reflected from the roof of the chamber. The previously solid concentrates become a molten mass in large vats through which waste material rises and is discarded as slag. What remains is poured into ingots, called anodes, or matte. The anodes are submerged in vats, and, by electrolysis, pure copper is deposited on a thin copper cathode. The metal is again melted and cast into bars ready for market.

The Lady knows that the historic Douglas Mansion, now an Arizona State Museum, is filled with history and samples of ore taken from Jerome. She knows that (spelled differently above) Lescher, Kibbey & Mahoney was the architectural firm that designed the Douglas Mansion and also created her. Her pride is tempered by the historic past of which she is so proud.

A New Look

Spring has arrived, and the trees are all leafing out. The hillside no longer looks so brown and bleak. All around the Lady, little purple flowers are blooming. They twist up and around the debris that is lying all around her. Harry and Walter have moved the old rose bushes from their home against the house to the perimeter of the rock walls, where they have taken hold, thanks to Walter's constant watering. New leaves are lining up along the stalks, and soon the bushes will bud and bloom. All over the terraces and the back hill, green things are shooting up through the dry leftovers of winter, reaching for the sun. The lilac bushes are budding, and the fruit trees are flowering. My green thumbs are itching to get into the dirt and do some planting; however, this is not the time to plant as there is much bulldozing and moving about of rocks and landscaping materials that still needs to take place.

Inside the house, the bare walls down to the lathe have all been cleaned out. All the old plaster, dirt and "stuff" is gone. Michael has cleared and vacuumed the walls, leaving the lathe clean and dirt free. We spoke about putting plaster back on the damaged walls but decided that drywall would be a better option. Bo, who has been a drywall man for years, has done all the taping and prep work. Now that the rooms are completed, he concocts a potion of sand, paint and who knows what else that is sprayed onto the drywall and has the feel and appearance of plaster. All the walls appear to be plastered again and look as they did in 1921. Reaching out gingerly to touch the texture of the walls, the Lady quickly draws her fingers back as she is startled by the roughness. "Oh my! It feels just like the original plaster," she thinks. Thanks to Bo's skill, the finish has been masterfully restored. Using his expertise, he has successfully textured flat walls into a finish that rivals that of the original.

In the dining room, new walls are in place. All the metal strappings and all the shoring up is now hidden behind wallboard. The living room and the guest room ceilings have lost their "popcorn" texture, and soon it will be time to paint. New wooden doors and windows are all gathered together in Walter's workroom awaiting installation. Old seeded glass will be put into the windows and door to make them look as they did in 1921. "I love the fresh spring air," muses the Lady. "There must be a way to keep the windows open for me."

Danny has nearly completed his electrical job, and my decision to have the living room ceiling fans employ an off/on pull chain delights him. He will wire these fans and lights so the lights will work from either side of the room, and the fans will be manually operated. He had worried about the difficult task of trying to get switches to handle all the variations in the rooms, so he is happy with my simple solution.

As Harry, Sam and I stand at the front door and look at the footings on the cement, we see the outline of a stoop much different than what exists now. I find an old photo of that side of the house at Paul and Jerry's Bar in town, and it appears that there was once a small covered roof along the west side of the house protecting the front door and the coal chute from weather damage. There are footings visible where pillars once held a narrow roof. More research is needed in this area.

The side vented evaporative cooler is conspicuous where it sits at the south end of the house, so Harry will build a low wall around it. This will be a great place to store a garden hose and a couple of garbage cans. Originally, I thought this was a great idea, but in reality, it didn't work at all and was totally removed. A utility sink will be installed inside the small garage bay, with another placed outside for outdoor gardening projects. The Lady sees all this progress and yet knows that there are still many months of hard work ahead. She itches with anticipation at getting everything done. Patience was not one of her virtues, nor is it one of mine.

It is a few weeks before I visit the Lady again, and the changes are exciting. The rock retaining wall on the west side of the house is down and will soon be rebuilt. Drywall now covers the ceilings, and as I watch Harry and Zack place the sheets into the gizmo that raises them to the ceiling for snug and tight placement, I am pleased with their skill and expertise. The Lady is now in new undergarments of white board, her modesty restored.

A large farmhouse sink sits in the kitchen, and the stove hood shines in bright stainless steel. The heavy plywood is ready for a template to be made for granite countertops that will be installed both in the kitchen and in the butler's pantry. The Lady remembers wonderful smells of baking bread and bubbling stew, and she can't wait for me to put on an apron, slice up the onions and carrots and get cooking. "What wonderful meals came from this kitchen, and what wonderful dinners we had when I was young. Good wine, good food and good company provided me with good memories and anticipation for future parties."

Looking at the architectural plans for the house, we realize some of our guesswork hasn't been completely accurate: a window where there once was a door; a series of steps now just a flat stoop; a small garage that is now a dirt hill. Should we redo our work or continue to work with what is already there? How significant are these subtle differences? Because we aren't sure, I am pleased that Harry, in his careful disassembly of the Lady, has not destroyed anything.

Most of the Lady stands today as she did in 1921, poised and beautiful. Most of the issues we were unsure of were resolved as she was undressed and her true self revealed. How lucky we've been to be able to preserve her. Interestingly enough, the plans reveal to us that there originally was not a small covered porch over the entry and the coal chute. Moreover, what we thought was the front of the house is actually the rear! Having the plans is certainly a boon.

Wood floors that were painted brown and covered with carpet now glow the color of honey. All the little nail holes and other small nicks and splits add character to this warm, inviting floor. Scott and his crew have done a wonderful job of bringing life back to what we salvaged of the old Douglas fir flooring. Scott's brother-in-law, John, will sand the cabinets and rid them of the many layers of paint they have acquired over the years. "I am so happy to have all this cheap makeup off my skin," the Lady croons. "I feel like I am having a wonderful facial and massage at the same time as John scrapes and sands all the many colors off my cabinets."

The decision is made to place trusses and create a new roofline. We also plan to add on a three-car garage that will match the house. Maybe someday we can rebuild the little garage back into the indentation still visible on the side of the hill. The driveway will be torn up and replaced with some type of paving stone instead of flagstone. Also, as the driveway is now about two feet higher than it was originally, it will be leveled somewhat, though it cannot go as low as it was initially due to new gas and water lines. Instead, a drainage channel will be designed and put in place so that water does not end up where it shouldn't. Old lilac and rose bushes, growing along what we now know is the *back* side of the house, will stay put, but we'll prune and trim them with care.

The ivy that has been home to many birds over the years is pulled from the side of the house. As the ivy tendrils let loose their grip, the original color of the house is revealed: The exterior was stuccoed in gray and accented with Douglas green trim. When the house was painted yellow, instead of taking down the ivy, the painters simply painted around it. The original blueprints also reveal that the house had shutters around all the windows, which led us to yet another important decision. Do we want to put them back up?

The crew from Cole Tile is preparing to finish the slate in the basement, and then Harry will finish the wall and make repairs downstairs in the cellar. Cole Tile comes with 52 years of experience in laying intricate stone and tile, and we've subcontracted with them to tile the bathroom and kitchen. Just this week, the tiles were ordered from Facings of America, and they should all arrive within two weeks.

It seems like we are on fast-forward now, compared to how slowly our work in prior months has progressed. The outside awaits new stucco and a new coat of paint. Warmer weather lends itself well to outdoor work, and as the rock retaining wall is rebuilt, our talk turns to fruit trees and bushes, an herb garden and a large oak tree, one of the few remaining live oak trees in the area. (Jerome was at one time a large oak forest and might appreciate a tribute to its history.)

The Lady takes a deep breath and spins around, looking at the many projects all going on simultaneously. She is overwhelmed by so many workers clamoring over her restoration. She is pushed, pulled and tugged here and there. She is being fitted with a completely new wardrobe and is looking forward to its completion, when she will again stand tall and stately in fashionable attire.

Reconstruction of the
Honeymoon Cottage Continues

*S*pring's cool has moved quickly into the hot summer for which Arizona is known. All living things suffer through this period of the year: prickly pear cactus pads are flat as pancakes for lack of water, and brown hillsides reflect the lack of rain. The Lady looks skyward at the build-up of the afternoon clouds, hoping they will release some much-needed moisture on the parched earth. Harry and Walter and the rest of the house crew arrive early in the morning before the heat is too unbearable. In the late morning, they move inside to work to escape the sun and heat. Afternoon shade from the reconstructed deck affords all of us the opportunity to sit and enjoy a cold drink. Listening carefully, the Lady hears the story of the piano theft and the Keyboard Gang, and she smiles as she remembers the musical evenings of a former family. It will be wonderful to hear music resounding again through her rooms.

Darin, who seems to relish the high temperatures, continues stacking the boulders and rocks as the wall winds its way north and eastward to the property line. Michael, back from an L.A. film project, works alongside Darin to stack the boulders and rock that make up the retaining wall. There are no more packrats, but scorpions run for cover as the boulders and rocks are knocked down and moved so the wall can be rebuilt. As Darin moves the rocks and boulders around, he discovers a large centipede, light pink in color, the length as long as the width of a large shovel. The insect is angry at being disturbed and raises up his head as if to attack. Darin drops him into a large glass bottle for me to release later. The sting from a centipede can leave a nasty wound.

Tops of old bottles, left intact after the bottles themselves were broken, are abundant in the ground. This area to the north of the house must have been used as a dumping ground or target practice area. Shooting at bottles balanced on top of the boulders was probably a favorite pastime long ago. An old wash is filled with smaller boulders to cut the water flow from a heavy rain so there will be no washout of soil. At the far end of the lawn, the wall will have a small terraced area with another wall up against the hillside. The yard now appears larger and more open as the wall leans into the hillside.

An area just north of the house where the garden will be planted is graded and is now free of debris and rocks. This area will be fenced in to keep out hungry animals that eat any greenery they can find. A very old, small grapevine, which has managed to hang on for dear life all these years, is denuded on a regular basis by some animal that finds it tasty.

David has finished the wood trim around most of the interior doorways, and Walter has many of the new old-style windows installed. The view from the kitchen through the widened doorway to the old porch provides a lovely picture of what will eventually become the flower and vegetable garden. Fresh vegetables and herbs will soon be planted; the Lady tries hard to recall the smells of sweet basil and oregano, rosemary and thyme, intermingled with roses, and lilacs. She imagines the soon-to-be bountiful garden surrounding her and longs for the orchard that once was fruitful. My joy of gardening has already been shared with her, and she looks forward to the day when I once again don my garden gloves.

The Lady looks out over the Verde Valley in amazement at the growth of homes and businesses. Having been bent over for so many years, she was unable to see what was happening right in front of her eyes. She is delighted that there is ample land around her and that her space allows her the freedom to breathe in all the redolence of the surrounding vegetation.

The deck is framed, and the new corbels are awaiting stucco. A surface on the deck has been spread, and the floor, which gently slopes toward the southeast end of the deck, will drain water into a scupper made of hammered copper. Walter found the original round scupper crushed and discolored under an old discarded water heater. He restored the copper tube to its original beauty, and the Lady is now satisfied with her beautiful new adornment. Stucco will soon be applied and the original metal railing set between the parapet walls. The house now awaits paint. Hangers at the end of each column will hold flower baskets, and a swing will hang between two columns. Closing her eyes, the Lady remembers enjoying gentle evening breezes while looking out over the valley lights and relishes the promise of new life.

Walter continues to work on the windows and doors and is ready to glaze the remainder of them. Soon, all the rotted windows and doors will be replaced.

The original window cranks were made of nickel-plated brass. They were hinged, and a small crank turned and opened or closed the window. As they were made of brass, a soft metal, the cranks wore down over the years with continued use. Some wouldn't even turn or would become stuck with the window open and water raining in or they were unable to open at all. As the cranks became more and more worn down over the years, many of the windows were simply nailed shut. I tried every shop I could find that might sell this older style of window cranks – I even called the original manufacturer, Russwin Crank in New England, who was still in business after these many years. I was told the company had not produced this type of window crank in over 50 years. I am sure the young fellow I spoke with thought I was crazy for trying to find old cranks when I could much more easily install newer windows and simpler openers. I was stymied. Either I must find the cranks somewhere or switch to another type of window. This would mean removing all of the original windows and going to a different design, something I considered a last resort.

Harry and Walter came to the rescue yet again. They knew of a machinist living in Jerome who had a machine shop in Clarkdale, a small town at the bottom of the hill beneath Jerome. Jay Misany was able to take one of the old window cranks and design and program his very sophisticated machinery to manufacture new window cranks out of stainless steel identical in shape and construction to the originals. The brushed stainless steel cranks even had the appearance of the original nickel-finished cranks. I had the opportunity to watch the complicated process as the new cranks were produced at Jay's shop. How fortunate I was to have found this talented machinist.

When he delivered all the cranks, the Lady stood in awe as Harry and Walter placed a new crank on each windowsill to await installation. The Lady grimaced as the old cranks were removed from her windows; many of the old screws were frozen into the wood after so many years and were difficult to unscrew. Some of the screws were so tight that they had to be drilled out. Determination and a burning desire to see the new cranks installed kept everyone motivated to get the job done.

Inside, work continues with Sam Cole of Cole Brothers Tile placing tumbled travertine walls in the bathrooms. Wainscot trim of a different color looks great. The original plaster in each bathroom had brick-shaped imprints pressed into the wet wall covering. Travertine, with its old look and variations of color, lends itself to a similar but more refined look. The backsplashes in the kitchen and butler's pantry are now completed with four-inch squares of ceramic field tiles. Cabinets will be reinstalled soon. We find many old wood boards with the name "Clinton Campbell" written on them in large script. Clinton must have been proud of his work on the Lady, signing his name everywhere, as was the custom of the day. (Much later we discovered that Clinton Campbell was a main worker that helped build the Lady).

The outside crew will soon move to the first level of the terrace and run the Bobcat through the trees, taking out the small sucker trees while leaving the larger trees intact. A clearing will become a walkway to a large mesquite tree that plays host to a sitting area. The entire first terrace wall must come down to be rebuilt. Through the years, it has collapsed, and large boulders have rolled down the hillside. This terrace wall must be rebuilt higher than before to retain the filled in yard. Steps at the north end of the yard will lead to the patio and walkway. Soon, work will begin on the second wall. It, too, will be taken down and rebuilt. A vineyard planted here will help hold the soil in place, and all the debris that has landed on the first and second levels will be cleared out after being "sifted." Garbage and grass cuttings, roofing materials, tin cans, broken glass, dishes and even old plumbing items were tossed over the terraces. The Lady, always tidy, will be pleased to have her yard cleaned up.

Plans are now drawn up for the garage, which will lose its ill-fitting Southwestern look, automatic doors and pop outs. A roofline to match the house and period-correct doors will provide a 1920s look. Soon, grass will encircle the house up to the garage, and a new gravel driveway will be spread. The Lady spins around, feeling giddy and effervescent at the transformation she is undergoing. She feels so happy and is looking forward to the near future, when she will again house a family who cares about her.

Summer Reverie

Warm weather arrives, and the apple tree, the apricot tree and the old rose bushes are in full bloom. There is an engaging honeyed essence in the air as the Lady takes a deep breath, savors the aroma and slowly exhales. All of the daily activities and the hustle and bustle of so many trades-people fulfilling their commitment to put her back together wear the Lady out. She still seeks to regain her strength, her stamina sorely tested in the teardown. The excitement and activity sap her energy, as she is used to reposing most of the day. Despite her exhaustion, she is thrilled with the process and eager to see what will happen next.

The sanding of the wood floors tickles her feet, and the dust from the grinders makes her sneeze. She marvels that all the old brown paint on the floors comes off so easily, the wood below left glowing with warmth. She loves the look and feel of wood and wonders why so many of her past houseguests covered up the floor with tiles, paint and carpet.

Granite countertops lay heavy on the strong wood cabi-netry in the kitchen and butler's pantry. Sinks and fixtures are installed with the promise they will soon carry water through the faucet. The stove hood is in place awaiting the arrival of the appliance that will occupy the space beneath it. Paint will be applied to the walls as soon as the trim wood is up, and then the walls will look finished.

The big tub is reset in the master bath thanks to the elbow grease of four strong men. This cast iron beauty from the '20s is old, big and has room to fit two people comfortably. It is deep and wide, and I am glad there is now the 75-gallon hot water heater with a re-circulating pump to fill it. This tub will require a lot of hot water for long, pleasant soaks. The Lady sighs and turns her head to look at the tub. She remembers many cold nights where a hot bath before bedtime was a long, relaxing end to a perseverant day. Lavender fragrance from the bath salts leaves a bouquet in the air that still lingers on the bath towels in the mornings. Lavender, a fragrance used often in the '20s, is again enjoying popularity today.

A little push against her backside takes the Lady by surprise. The columns for the deck are being set. She has been squinting every morning for weeks now as the sun rises, beaming through the French doors into the living room with uncompromising brightness. The columns and the deck they will support will soon shade her eyes, and she relishes the thought that cool shade will soon be available.

The attic breathes now as vents have all been opened and screened. Air now flows freely around the Lady's head. From head to toe, she feels invigorated and alive and looks forward to each new day, always wondering what will happen next.

Rock walls that have held the hill at bay at the front of the house are now being torn down by the backhoe. Zach Dreuen, another local from Jerome, and Darin rebuild the wall into a well-angled work of "wall art" that differs greatly from the bulging pregnant walls that were there before. Gravity and washout have left the walls just barely standing, home to another family of packrats burrowed in crevices and tunnels. The wall breaking apart sends rat mothers running frantically up the hillside, babies clinging precariously to their underbellies. By afternoon, the gopher snakes are moving in, slithering in and out of the rat nests, seeking left-behind babies on which to feast. The food chain works well in all circumstances, and the snakes take advantage of the situation to keep the rat population under control.

Outside, the sound of a jackhammer wakens the Lady with a start. For a moment she is frightened, thinking that someone is attacking her very foundation and destroying her sturdy walls. She turns toward the vibrating loud noise and sees a young man leaning on what looks like a large steel stick with a bar across the top. The jackhammer is jumping up and down, throwing dirt, rocks and dust all over the place. "They will soon discover what has been hidden for over thirty years," the Lady thinks as the old cement driveway is broken up. Soon, another secret will be revealed. Sure enough, steps are still there leading up to the front door. The story of the buried steps is indeed an interesting one.

The Great Storm of 1967

The winter of '66 and '67 left Jerome and the Verde Valley with an inordinate amount of snow. Cleopatra Hill was covered for most of the winter with a thick blanket of the heavy wet stuff. As spring slowly pushed winter aside and warmer temperatures began to melt the snow, soil on the surrounding hills became saturated with the runoff. As if this was not bad enough, spring rains soon arrived. The soil absorbed all it could, but one day the whole hillside couldn't take anymore and just let loose. The Lady watched in amazement and fear as boulders, rocks and all kinds of vegetation began moving down the hill behind her.

A small one car garage, tucked into the hillside, that sat just off the south end of the house resisted the force of water, mud and debris as long as it could, but the deluge proved to be too much in the end. With a sigh of resignation, it let loose of its foundation and slid slowly across the driveway, propelled by the force. Picking up speed as it moved across the lawn, it raced to its demise over the two terraces and down the hill to a wash at the end of the property. The Lady watched in horror as the little building she loved closed its eyes and gave in at last to the inevitable force of nature.

She feared for her own existence as the storm continued on through the night. Falling into a fitful sleep, she awoke at daybreak to find 20 inches of slippery mud covering her lovely grass lawn and the four steps leading into the house. She was grateful the mud had not come up higher than her petticoats and wondered how her family would manage to clean up the mess. As she sadly predicted, they did as always and covered up the damage instead of repairing it. Soon there was a new cement driveway where there once was green grass. The steps were buried under the new driveway, and now, because the level of the land was higher, rain run-off drained into her basement leaving the Lady's feet cold and wet. A musty odor permeated her clothing, perpetuated by the moisture that lay beneath her flooring for weeks on end until evaporation finally carried it away. She missed her little garage friend and was lonely for the conversations and stories they shared of the comings and goings of the household. She thought often of his early demise and how the garage seemed to give up its life too easily. "Never will I just surrender so easily to outside forces," she vowed.

In the future, the Lady would think of these words as she was beaten, bloodied, ignored and mistreated. She held on to the hope that someone would rescue her someday and never malign her again. It would be many years after the great rain, and her resolve would be tried and tested repeatedly, before she would be rescued. It is a tribute to her tenacity that she did indeed hold on, even when the future looked bleak at best. But hang on she did, slowly slipping away into obscurity, but still hoping. She remembers so many wonderful years before she was left to languish and decay. A tear of happiness slips down her cheek as she now envisions a future of guardianship with love.

Welcome Surprises

*J*uly slides slowly into August as summer unsheathes one more month of heat. As the monsoon season moves in, cooler weather is yet another four to six weeks away. The torrid humidity in the air makes it difficult for any of us to be composed and comfortable. The promise of fall and its cooler weather is appealing.

Activity around the edge of the yard captures the Lady's attention. As she watches with widened eyes, the many small trees and shrubs that border her eastern property line fall. The strength of heavy equipment rattles her shutters as the Bobcat we rented cuts a distinct line of access along the first retaining wall to the northern edge of the lawn. For a brief moment, the Lady is dismayed by all of the activity. However, her consternation is quickly dispelled as she recognizes something that has long been hidden under the debris. Years ago, this first terrace was built as a retaining wall for the yard, and roses were planted along its edge. Fruit trees were abundant at the southern edge of the yard. Without hesitation, apple and apricot trees released their bounty in the early summer.

Harry runs the little Bobcat along the rock wall, and all

the debris and grass cuttings, tin cans, glass and garbage reveal themselves. Eighty years of having to live with so much trash in her lap and under her feet brings tears to the Lady. It was so easy for her prior occupants to throw all the unwanted items over the hill rather than disposing of them properly in the landfill. She stares as Harry salvages pieces of glass and pottery. He soon has a collection of many years' worth of eclectic "stuff." Piece after piece is retrieved and stacked on the lawn table, now laden with forgotten treasure. As Harry continues his grading, he spies a small pair of gold frame reading glasses that once perched on someone's nose. One can only wonder what eyes have looked through these lenses.

The excess dirt is pushed over the edge of the second terrace wall to build up the walkway that has washed away over the years. The first terrace wall proves to be in extremely good condition. The large boulders on the bottom part of this 13-foot high dry stack wall weigh in at 600 to 800 pounds each. They were placed as part of the wall using a small crane that was attached to a special narrow gauge track mine car borrowed from one of the mine tunnels. The car then moved on a temporary track lain on the access road to build the walls. The little train car would bring in the boulders; the crane and several men would lift each boulder, turn and hoist it up and place the rock securely in place. Today, all that remains of the track are some rusty nails. Other than a few places where the wall washed out, the boulders are still where they were originally set. Those old timers sure knew how to build rock walls, even without a Bobcat.

As more dirt is moved over the second terrace, the road widens, and another wall appears. One can only access this area from each end of the yard. "Soon," the Lady thinks, "I will have no more secrets to reveal, and my story can be retold."

Later in the week, Harry, Walter, John McLoughlin (my son) and I walk to the lower levels of the property to tag trees that will be spared from the Bobcat's bucket. The large mesquite trees will be pruned, and small scrub brush taken out. The old shake shingle roof from an earlier hat the lady wore many years ago when her copper was removed and sold and that has lain for over 10 years in a pile will be hauled away. Who knows what wonderful keepsakes will be found as this area is scraped and the surface moved about. Today I found an old pottery crock, a small white glass jar and several ancient bottles, their former contents remaining a mystery.

Inside, Danny Rowley has just about completed the rewiring. The basement has bright lighting from fluorescent ceiling lights, and the old line for the bell on the back patio has been rediscovered. Two new outlets located on the outside of the house will provide electricity, which will be run to the edge of the yard so an electrical fence can be installed to keep the deer, cattle and javalina from devouring all the vegetation. The low voltage does not injure the animals, rather it merely surprises them and keeps them away from the yard.

I meet with Bo (Robert Wilson, master painter) to consult with him on the paint. Bo will do all the remaining prep work on the wood surfaces before applying new paint. Windows and doors have already been primed by Walter and David, so new paint will be easy to apply. Old surface paint will be sanded off, and the wood will be re-primed so the new paint will be even and smooth.

Luckily, the original wood cabinetry still remains in the kitchen, the butler's pantry, (adjacent to the kitchen), the bathrooms and the closets. The kitchen has cabinets reaching to the ceiling with plenty of shelving. There are sliding bread boards and drawers in all of the cabinets. The countertops are painted wood. Many counters in the '20s had curtains hanging to the floor, which were attached under the countertops. Needed items were stored behind the curtain under the counter. The master bathroom has a closet and built-in drawers, and the master bedroom has built-in, his and hers closets of assorted sizes, all with built-in drawers of their own. In the kitchen there are several bins, some large and some small, lined with galvanized metal. These were used to hold grains, beans and other items used in baking and cooking. Remember, this was a time prior to convenient packaged mixes and prepared food.

The screened-in porch had a hook attached up high near the ceiling where a smoked ham would hang, and eggs and butter were kept in the small root cellar in the floor. A pulley attached to the ceiling allowed a small metal basket that held perishables to be raised and lowered from this small cistern. In many places, this room was called a mud porch and would be used in a similar manner.

The builders of the Honeymoon Cottage had the benefit of adequate funds for building the best and most modern home. Most of the homes in Jerome did not have closets, built-in drawers, large kitchens where food was cooked or baked or a butler's pantry for preparing the food before it was served to the family. The family that lived in the Honeymoon Cottage always ate their meals in the large dining room. Many of the homes in Jerome were small square structures, and some had wood burning stoves for cooking and heating. The Honeymoon Cottage has thick brick walls covered outside with cement stucco and inside with lathe and plaster, whereas most other houses in Jerome were simple wooden structures with no insulation. The Lady shivers as she remembers seeing her neighbors bundled up in layers of clothing in an attempt to stay warm for the few months of winter.

Harry and Walter have pulled all the kitchen cabinets away from the walls. Now they have all-new backing and have been reinstalled in the kitchen and the butler's pantry. When the interior work is completed, toilets, sinks and tubs will be set, and Robert will finish the plumbing. A new gas line is scheduled to be installed by the gas company; the 80-year-old line is definitely overdue for attention.

The Lady admires Harry as the orchestra director who has successfully brought so many musicians together in harmony. Just when everyone is playing on key, hammers begin pounding on her head to install the new roof. How does Harry hold it all together and keep everyone organized and on task? The Lady sees his skill and expertise, and she knows and understands from personal experience over these past months why I have so much confidence in his ability and why I value his opinion and listen to his advice on the restoration.

Roofing companies have provided quotes for a new head dressing for the Lady, and a decision will be made soon. Gutters and downspouts are being fabricated, and the present brown roof will be removed or topped off with new blue architectural shingles.

The original plans for the Lady called for a shingle roof, but someone decided that copper would look better, and there was certainly no shortage of copper in the area. Tons of pure copper were placed on her head, though the only copper remaining is on a small overhang by the powder room. The rest of the roof was removed and sold when copper prices were high. A pale yellow exterior paint with soft blue trim will brighten up the Lady's dress and match her new blue hat. Brick chimneys, exposed after the old stucco was chipped off, will look great next to the blue roof.

The old cement patio, nestled under the deck, is jackhammered up. New cement and travertine will cover the patio and stairs leading out from the dining room. Soft yellow and blue stone will complement the new house color.

If you are quiet and listen, you can hear the Lady giggle as she looks at the small 4×4 French tiles hand-painted by the David Day Studio in Texas. Twenty-two of these tiles adorn the walls in the small powder room off the foyer. Each tile with a French caricature is accompanied by its English translation. Step in and learn a little French while you are there.

Sammy Cole has applied the tiles to even the smallest of the bathrooms. "What a clever addition to the powder room," the Lady thinks. Field tile will surround randomly placed decorative tiles.

Darin Lewis, a townie and Jack of All Trades, continues to work on rebuilding the rock terrace walls, ignoring the heat as he moves from terrace to terrace. He has become the resident wall expert, selecting just the right boulders. The rocks must be set in such a way that they will stay in place without mortar, allowing water to percolate through them without washing out the soil behind. Darin has become very skilled and can spot just the rock he needs from quite a distance.

Paul Hughes, from Cheshire Cat Pest Control, visits the Lady and lends his expertise to exterminate creepy crawlies prior to installing the new insulation. He also sets bait traps for the packrats. Exiled from their nests, we don't want these critters to make new homes in the garage among the furniture and bedding being stored. Harry chuckles as we see a furry gray packrat run from one burrow in the rock wall to another. One can only wonder how many bright objects and long lost items these little guys have carried off to be stored forever in their tunnels and niches. They are fun to watch, but they can be very destructive. With such prolific reproduction, they quickly take over if not controlled.

Work continues as summer moves on, and we all anticipate a completion date and cooler weather sometime in October. The Lady takes a deep breath and sighs as she looks around herself. Although she is still torn asunder, she knows that everything will eventually come together, her new dress being tailored for a perfect fit. She hears talk of a wedding to be held in the spring, and she is happy at the thought of a celebration of love. Her heart warms to know that she will play host to the family and friends of the happy couple.

Only in Jerome

A longtime friend of mine died on July 4. Selecting a sympathy card for the family was difficult. You can't get too mushy about the former chief of police of Seattle, but my condolences were heartfelt. A card depicting a rust-colored dragonfly along with an appropriate verse was sent to his niece and nephew on Thursday, July 18. In the late afternoon of July 19, as Harry and I stood on the lawn, a large rust-colored dragonfly landed at eye level, on the wall of the house, right next to us. The next day, as I visited with Andrea Prince, owner of the Surgeons House Bed and Breakfast in town, the same rust-colored dragonfly appeared in her yard as I walked across the lawn. The large insect lingered for a bit, looking at us, before flying off across the yard. Neither Harry or Andrea had ever, in all the years they have been in Jerome, seen a dragonfly of such a color and size.

The Good, the Bad and the Ugly

*L*ight comes later in the morning now, and Harry and the workers arrive later than just a few weeks ago. As the sun rises over the ridge, it seems more intense and directs its rays right into the eyes of the awakening Lady.

Work continues at a fast pace with workers in all areas of the house at what seems like all hours of the day. The outside stucco has been repaired and is ready for painting. A once-hidden second chimney, all brick, is exposed by Zack as the old stucco is chipped off. In better condition than its brother at the other end of the house, it stands now as a duplicate sentinel on the roof. The copper trim and the blue shingles for the roof arrive, and Richard Peek will soon balance them on the Lady's steeply pitched roof to install her new blue hat. The completion of the restoration is in sight, although it is still months ahead, and we know that problems might yet arise that could set us back.

The first terrace wall has turned into an ugly challenge. Parts of the rock wall were in extremely good condition for being 80-plus years old, while other parts further south along the wall had fallen apart. Clearing the debris of so many years, Harry finds pieces of the original cement columns from the deck that have been integrated with the boulders and are now a part of the wall. Again, the Lady reveals her true self to Harry as he uncovers evidence of a stairway and walkway at the south end of the first terrace. This section is in need of such extensive reconstruction that Harry decides to wait to tackle this obstacle.

The yard above the first terrace is now filled with dirt to raise the yard to the top of the first wall, with just a slight grade to prevent flooding when it rains. The zenith of this first terrace, 12 feet high in some places, made rebuilding it very difficult. Mike and Darren worked primarily while standing on scaffolding and a tall ladder, carrying one rock at a time. Sometimes the rock would fit well, other times not, and sometimes it had to go back to the rock pile to await placement in another area.

Packrats still in residence scurry here and there, frantically racing in and out of the wall as their nests are disturbed. It is backbreaking and very labor-intensive work, yet rebuilding this part of the yard is essential. As the backhoe clears the dead vegetation and removes years of debris, the area reveals a small road that runs alongside the second wall. Plans, that seem to change on a day-to-day basis, now include creating a walking trail, complete with rest areas placed throughout the lower level of land. Much work remains in that area, and my son John will shop for a small tractor to accomplish the task. As the Lady watches and listens, she is amazed at all of the new technology that provides mechanical help for jobs that were all done by hand in the past.

Feeling a sudden rush of outside air, the Lady turns and sees her dining room window tugged and pushed from its framework. The window was badly corroded with water stains, and a large crack ran from one corner to the other. The new window moves carefully from a wooden rack into its new frame with the help of Harry, Walter and John. The visibility through the clean glass immediately improves the beauty of the view from the dining room window. The maid's room also receives new double-paned glass. Housed in a handmade wooden crate, the two large glass windows made the trip to Jerome safely from the Phoenix flatlands.

A large wooden beam meant for the garage ceiling arrives and is set aside for use in a few weeks as the garage undergoes its makeover. It will eventually support a new 7×12 pitch roof. The structure's clashing Southwest design will be redesigned to match the Lady's French country style. A dormer will be built above the garage, complete with sleeping quarters and a bathroom. Downstairs in the garage, two bathrooms, with both inside and outside entry, will be installed in the east end of the first bay. Also, an outside sink with a flex-hose shower will be a great addition to facilitate cleanup after outdoor chores.

Inside, the painting continues, but the job proves too much for just one person. Bo will move on to another job, and Eric Morice of Platinum Painting will bring in a crew to complete the Lady's makeup. All the window panels must be painted by hand. With so many window panes, the job is very labor intensive. Eric has a large crew and will complete the coloring of the Lady, both inside and out, within a few weeks.

The tile in the small powder room is complete, and "une petite leçon de Francais" (a small French lesson) awaits its first visitor. Boxes of extra field tile sit in the closet awaiting the building of the small bathrooms in the garage. Tile had been ordered from David Day Studios in Texas to reach up to the ceiling in this quaint little bath, but a decision to go only halfway up the wall makes more sense. What to do with all the extra tile? The Lady scratches her head, and when a decision is made to install two bathrooms in the garage, she knows this excellent tile will be put to good use.

Danny is ready to install all the light fixtures and anxiously awaits the completion of the interior painting. The Lady also awaits the removal of all the bare light bulbs hanging on wires throughout the house. These bulbs have provided illumination, but they are certainly not becoming to a Lady of such stature.

"Coming to see me?" The Lady eavesdrops on a conversation between Mary Wills and myself. Mary is a friend and owner of Nellie Bly, a wonderful Kaleidoscope shop on Main Street. A sister group of philanthropic/social ladies in Sedona has been invited by the Jerome group for lunch and a visit to the Honeymoon Cottage. A group of 60 "Women of Sedona," will tour Jerome, hosted by the "Ladies of Jerome," on October 15. The Lady wishes her restoration were complete but knows she will put her best face forward on this day regardless of her condition. "I won't be as lovely as I will be soon, but I will hold my head high," she says. "They will catch our vision, I'm sure. This is a wonderful opportunity for others to see what can be done when the heart is in the right place and caring people love an old, abused Lady and are able to see past her scars into the future."

Free Piano

*J*erome, Arizona, population 400, (give or take a few folks), abounds in stories of mysterious happenings and weird phenomena. The residents of this old mining town, their homes hanging on for dear life to the side of Cleopatra Hill, take all the ghost stories and strange occurrences in stride. Here's another story that makes people say, "Only in Jerome."

A small sign posted on the community bulletin board at the post office seems too good to be true. It reads: "FREE PIANO – Needs Home, Needs Tuning. Black Upright, Ornamental. You Remove."

I thought this piano might be perfect for the Honeymoon Cottage's decor. The Lady might welcome its melodious sounds. I call the number on the note. "The piano is on the porch," said a woman named Sally. "Just come and pick it up!" My son had seen the piano sitting on the porch of a house on Center Street, and he gave me directions for getting there. I made arrangements for Harry and Walter and three other men to go pick up the piano from the porch and bring it back to the house. They did just that, placing the piano in the garage.

The next day, I received a call from the Jerome Chief of Police, Allen Muma. A report had been filed about a stolen piano that was supposedly stashed in my garage. Seems like a neighbor had seen the five men take the piano off the porch and load it into a truck. The piano, however, had been purchased by a Jerome resident and was to be picked up on Tuesday, the same day that Harry and Walter and the "Keyboard Gang" had removed it from the porch.

This story might have ended right there with me going to jail as a piano thief were it not for Chief Muma's detective work. There were two pianos, both black uprights, both needing tuning, both sitting on the front porch and both to be picked up on Tuesday. The difference was that they were located exactly one street apart, in line with one another. The free piano was on Verde Street, and the "stolen" piano was on Center Street. Pat Jacobsen bought the upright that was on Julie Perkins' porch for pickup on Tuesday, the same day the Keyboard Gang struck and took the wrong piano.

Later: The sold piano was returned to the porch on Center Street by the Keyboard Gang; the free piano was picked up from the porch on Verde Street. Everybody was happy, especially me, as I did not relish the thought of doing time in jail.

Old Jerome photo shows the Honeymoon Cottage at far middle right of photo.

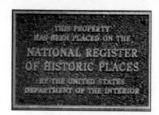

Plaque stating the status of the house.

Photo of house appearance when I bought it. (Note plywood roof over patio where now is the deck – also note cracks in structure.)

Santa Fe style "step-child" garage.

Original kitchen cabinets.

Butler's pantry.

Old gas boiler; old water heater.

John (Marge's son) looking at basement mess (note old coal burning boiler).

Pit where coal burning boiler once stood, that also filled with water when water heater leaked.

Dining room showing cracks and cracked plaster.

Dining room showing large cracks high on wall.

Upstairs sun room with cracked plaster and cracks in walls.

Outside wall cracks on front of house.

*House showing cracks, missing deck and building being
shored up after new foundation had been poured.*

Mikey in kitchen, showing original lathe.

Original radiators ready for placement in the house.

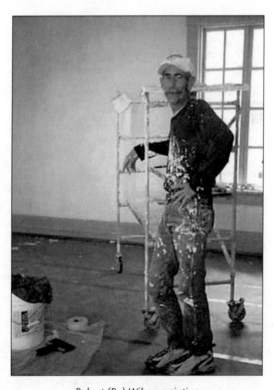

Robert (Bo) Wilson, painting

Marge's Mom Paula Heinemann (now deceased), looking at all the work on the house, as the west wall comes down, thanks to the backhoe.

Front stoop and stairs exposed as old cement driveway is torn up.

David Skimin planing wood trim for the house.

Jay Misany at his machine shop, working on the stainless steel window cranks.

Walter Aker, neighbor, townie, master wood worker,
builder and assistant to Harry Stewart.

Darin Lewis re-building the west dry stack wall.

Carrie, (Marge's daughter), playing air guitar with the re-built copper scupper.

Lucky (Blue Tick Hound) and Copper (Australian Shepherd) at home in Jerome.

Helper to Sam Cole, Cole Brothers Tile,
laying slate on the basement floor

Bobcat doing its job leveling the terraces
and carrying rocks for the wall rebuilds.

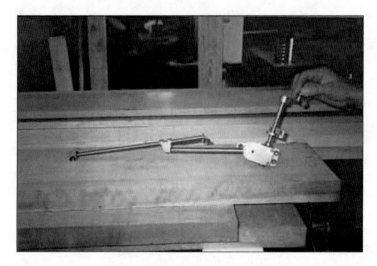

New stainless steel window cranks.

*John, (Marge's son), and Harry Stewart, General
Contractor, making plans for the grading.*

Kitchen with now exposed brick chimney, brass wall tiles behind Viking Stove and Viking refrigerator on right.

Far North rock wall with abundant blooming roses.

New pillars and old claw foot tub sitting on lawn.

Carrie as a guide for the visiting Sedona women.

New ceiling fixture in the dining room.

New cherrywood front door that Walter Aker built, with seeded glass windows.

Harry Stewart speaking with Phil Wright, (General contractor and builder) about the little house.

Old Santa Fe Style garage being torn apart and demolished.

Ed Gonzales wiring the Little House.

Sally Gonzales wiring the Little House (yes, they are a husband/wife team of licensed electricians).

Little House roofed, with new doors and almost painted.

Abe Stewart, (Harry's nephew), taking a well deserved break.

Leo Shakespeare pulling garden cart full of rosemary plants to line the yard.

Darin Lewis and Leo Shakespeare laying down the sprinkler system.

Robert Rose (plumber), and Scotty Nesselrode (gardener and saver of large trees), just as they had completed assembling the shed.

Piles of sod.

Marge checking out the little fruit trees.

Victor Senne (tile setter) and helpers, laying the travertine on the patio.

The 'old' Iron Maiden.

*Irme Obermeir (friend, and owner of
Windows by Design), hanging window trim and curtains.*

Darin, laying the stepping stones Harry made from extra cement.

The whole "famm damily" at the wedding.

Carrie and the dogs at the Home Tour.

Carrie dressed as the runaway bride for the Home Tour.

The house, as it looked for the Jerome Home Tour.

*Dorothy Miller, longtime resident of Jerome,
and I, when her home was on the Home Tour.*

Dorothy Miller and I, when my home was on the Jerome Historic Home Tour.

Lucky, and Scotty Nesselrode taking care of the yard.

Jerome volunteer firefighters at the site of the plane crash.

Iris blooming against dry stack wall.

Audrey elevator (also called A-frames) at the entrance to the Little Daisy Mine.

Two of the large Ponderosa Pines that Scotty saved.

*Storm over the Verde Valley – viewed from the
front yard of the Honeymoon Cottage.*

Christmas in Jerome.

Jerome, Arizona

Visit Jerome, an Arizona treasure, where the entire town is a National Historic Landmark

- Famous Historic Billion Dollar Mining Town
- Original Buildings from the Victorian Era through the 1920's
- Artist Colony with Over 30 Art Galleries and Studios
- Unique Shops
- Great Food
- Charming Lodging
- Museums and Historical Archives
- Stunning Vistas
- Special Events Throughout the Year

Experience Jerome!

Jerome Winery

Built on the side of Cleopatra Hill, between Prescott and Sedona in the town of Jerome.

OPEN DAILY
CALL FOR SEASONAL HOURS

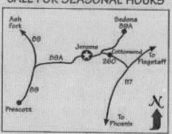

Jerome is a living historic mining town that has become an eclectic art community with many artisans, shops, restaurants, hotels and bed and breakfasts.

We feature hand crafted wines, hors d'oeuvres, and nostalgia in an enjoyable setting overlooking the beautiful Verde Valley and Sedona.

Jerome Winery offers private tastings, winemaker dinners, weddings, and special events.

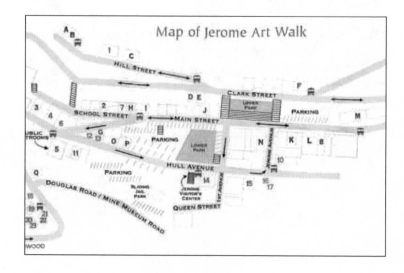

Map of Jerome Art Walk

Putting on a New Face
with a New Hat

*C*ooler mornings and less daylight keep everyone working all day now. The hot, humid days that seemed to wring
the starch out of everyone are now but a thing of the past.
Perfect weather greets all the busy hands at the Honeymoon
Cottage as more and more pieces of the Lady's history come
together.

The rush is on. There is no more time to take a day off
or find something else to do. The wedding is scheduled for
April 12, 2003, and everything must be perfect by then. The
Lady must be completely redressed, her yard laid with sod.
The fruit trees, shrubs and other plantings must all be in the
ground with a watering system in place. The garage's face-
lift must be completed and the wrought iron fence welded
and installed. There's so much to do in what now seems like
such a short time.

Harry feels the pressure and worries about whether or
not he will have enough help to get everything done. Jerome
often works on its own time, and its residents march to their
own drummers. "Rush" is not a part of the community's

vocabulary. Despite the looming deadline, I know that everything will fall into place as planned and reassure Harry that we will work toward the goal the best we can.

Three rock terrace walls now stand tall and solid. Harry continues cleaning out the areas along these walls. Remnants of an old shingle roof from the Lady's unfortunate past are scooped up and carried to the huge onsite dumpster and will eventually be hauled to the landfill. More evidence of the forlorn little garage is found below the hill, along with parts of the rock wall that were taken along as it made its way across the driveway and down the hill. All this debris is hauled off.

If the lowest terrace wall is not sound, pressure is placed on the second terrace wall. This, in turn, causes problems for the first terrace wall. The structures must be like a pyramid; each level supporting the level above it. Areas adjacent to the rock walls will be laid with sod to become large grass patios and walking areas. These walls proved to be more time consuming than any of us had imagined, but, like so many projects with the Lady, once it began, it could not be stopped. Building these walls has been well worth the time, effort and cost. Small seedlings have taken hold in the wall, and they wind around the rocks' odd shapes, grabbing hold wherever there is soil. Their roots will help stabilize the walls in the future and prevent erosion.

Soft yellow paint now covers the stark white of the primer on the outside of the house. Inside, the rooms are dimly lit; the windows are all covered with paper and tape to keep paint off the panes. The floors are covered with plastic that has been taped securely to the baseboards, and the inside windows are also papered and taped. Soon the inside will also be painted.

Outside, critters leave several animal trails throughout

the property. Deer, javelina, skunks, raccoons, rabbits and foxes move from one feeding area to another. The flowers and plants prove tasty to them.

The Lady raises her shoulders and wraps her arms around herself as she attempts to hold on to the warmth of the day's sunshine. All new valves have arrived for the radiators. They are cleansed and await painting. The valves will be installed, and the radiators will be placed back in the house after they are painted. Cooler weather is just around the corner, and the Lady feels the need for a little warmth early in the morning when the air is a tad nippy. The warmth of the day's sunshine lingers through the evening but dissipates during the night. The radiators will hold an even temperature through the night into the morning with a slow and even heat that is thermostatically controlled.

It's time for the new boiler to replace the old leaking boiler that supplied half of the radiators. Several small baseboard heaters that never worked well were hooked up in error to the hot water heater. The new system will connect all the radiators through a new gas boiler in the basement.

The Lady revels in her newfound self and awaits the new shutters that will grace her windows. Copper gutters will both accentuate and keep the rain out of her eyes. Fall rains have already pounded on her roof and settled all the dust from the 162-plus loads of fill dirt that Harry has hauled to the front yard to level it with the wall.

As she admires everything done, undone, redone and in the process of being done, the Lady overhears a most disturbing conversation: Her stepchild to the south will be demolished. The thought of the bulldozer and the backhoe taking down the garage alarms her. She never liked the Santa Fe style of the three-bay garage, but she has grown somewhat attached to it over the years nonetheless. She never considered the possibility that it might not be redressed.

She listens and learns that Blue Boelter, a local architect, will design the new building. Harry, whose careful, loving hands have torn the Lady apart and put her back together again, is too backlogged with work to handle the new building of the garage. Phil Wright, a well respected local builder, will rebuild the garage in likeness of the Lady, truly as a child of her own.

The Southwestern style garage that stands now next to the Lady was built by the previous owner on land that was once an orchard. The construction was never in keeping with the French country style of the house. At first, I had hoped to remodel the garage into a structure that would match the look of the house and build an addition upstairs. However, the structure would not accommodate the added weight of a second story and the decision was made instead to demolish the building and build a new, stronger garage.

Plans for the garage makeover arrive, and Blue Boelter has done a wonderful job. Like Harry, she understands old homes. She incorporates modern ideas with traditional charm, melding them together successfully. The garage will lose its flat roof, its pop outs around the windows and the three electrical garage doors and become a small accompaniment to the Lady. Several dormers with windows will bring light to the new guest room above the garage. A bath upstairs and lots of storage space will soon follow. Stairs will lead down from the deck along the backside of the garage.

Under the stairway, a door will open to a short hallway that leads to a men's room and a separate ladies' room. The entire rebuild will be wonderful, providing a changing room for brides and bridesmaids in one bay of the garage and leaving two bays for vehicles. The drab electric doors will be replaced with stylish double doors much like garage doors in the '20s. The roofline will match the house. Harry will not demolish the garage until the Lady herself is completely redressed. I am anxious to get started.

The Lady hums softly as I walk through the kitchen. I feel her peace and contentment in spite of all the stress she has been through in the last ten months. She is far more patient than I. Wisdom has come from her age, and she has endured misfortune for so many years. She provides us all with the perfect example of how to live. Soon, both she and I will relax as the restoration nears completion and she shines again as the Jewel of Jerome.

Asylum Roasted Butternut Squash Soup

*F*all is just around the corner. As cooler weather arrives, we look forward to tasty hot soups. This recipe comes from the delicious repertoire of Chef Richard D. Pasich, executive chef/partner of the Asylum Restaurant in Jerome. The Asylum is located in the Grand Hotel, one of the former hospitals atop Cleopatra Hill.

The original recipe, which will produce two mouth-watering gallons of soup, will serve a lot of hungry people. Don't worry – Chef Richard has adjusted the amounts for you. Enjoy! This soup is truly wonderful.

INGREDIENTS:

2 large whole butternut squash – roasted

1 white onion – chopped

2 each poblano peppers or green chili equivalent – roasted, peeled

6 ounces Oak Creek Amber beer or similar

2 cups vegetable stock

½ cup brown sugar

1 tablespoon garlic – minced
1 pinch cinnamon
1 pinch nutmeg
1 serrano chili – minced fine
1 cup heavy cream, salt and pepper to taste

PREPARATION METHOD:
Cut the squash in half and remove the seeds. Place
in shallow roasting pans with water and roast at 400
until very tender, apx. 45 minutes or more. Remove
from oven and cool. Roast, peel and de-seed poblano
chiles. Preheat skillet until scorching hot. Saute onions and chilies, then deglaze with beer. Add chicken
stock, peeled squash, and remaining ingredients except for the cream. Simmer together for 30 minutes
then puree. Remove from heat and slowly fold in the
heavy cream.

Source: "The Asylum Restaurant. Jerome,
Arizona" © 2002 Fools On The Hill Inc.

Next time you are in Jerome, stop by the Asylum and try
this wonderful soup. I know you will like it and want to
rush home immediately and cook up a batch for yourself.
Invite the neighbors and share this wonderful recipe with
them, as I do with mine. When the evenings are cool, it is
wonderful to have a hearty soup, fresh bread and a glass of
wine for dinner. One of the neighbors always brings along
an apple pie for dessert. This is the way Jerome works. It is
a small town of neighborly people who enjoy good food,
good company and good times.

Dusty Days, Windy Afternoons and Sudden Showers

Small particles of dust hang in the air as Scott McMillan runs his sander over the old Douglas fir floors. Scott has been visiting the Lady off and on for the past few months and is now a welcome guest. When the Lady first lost her dining room floor to the settled part of the front house, it was Scott who laid her new floor. When the rotted flooring in the bathrooms (yes, in all four of them) was pulled out, it was Scott who laid the new flooring. When the living room, the master bedroom upstairs, the landing, the kitchen floor and the sun room needed refinishing, it was Scott who tenderly rubbed the Lady's feet.

With time running short and the garage about to come down, Scott arrives late in the day to finish the final sand and apply the final finish. The sander moves lightly over the floor, creating very fine specks of wood weighing so little that gravity does not pull them out of the air quickly. They hover like a veil of luminous silt that sways to and fro with the slightest movement of air. Slowly and gently, these minute specks float to the floor, settling in small piles in corners of the room.

Earlier in the process of refinishing the floor, Scott used a rough sander, now followed by this smooth sander. Paint, dirt, glue and an accumulation of 80 years of wax and paint is removed by able hands and flooring equipment. Prior to the finish being applied, a hand rubbed across the floor double checks that all the fairy dust is gone and the wood is ready for the finish application. The first coat brings new life to the wood, whose grain now stands out with definition. The second coat brings out a warm honey color with a soft gloss that is most pleasing to the eye. Filler made of wood dust, glue and stain have taken care of cracks and splits. Various areas of the floor show a dark pattern of nail holes from prior "cover-up" flooring. The patterns remain after sanding, adding extra character to the floor.

The Lady sneezes as Scott vacuums up the dust puddles from the corners of the living room. The view out the French doors was hazy from so much dusty debris in the air, but a clear view of the Valley now greets the Lady, and she admires the red rocks of Sedona in the distance. These days, her head is held high under her new blue hat. Her soft yellow dress with new blue framed windows shows off her new trim figure. No more does she sag in the midsection. Neglect and cover-ups are no longer a part of her life; loving care now accentuates everything. Her basement petticoats once stained and dirty are now painted white and are clean and tidy. The stagnant water that once collected in the basement pit where the coal-burning boiler sat accumulates no more. A level floor made of beautiful slate covers the old cracked cement floor, and fluorescent light bulbs now illuminate the room.

Upscale fixtures representative of the '20s hang in each room. Sconces in the living room and dining room emit a soft, pleasant light. Ceiling fans in each room await specialty light kits that are on order, and an elegant, ornate chandelier in the dining room is anxious to light up a family supper. The Lady appreciates that harsh, bright lighting is discouraged by alabaster glass globes and shades that wrap around flattering soft light bulbs. What a difference the new fixtures make. Antique copper switch plates take her back to the '20s. The servants' bell system, from the dining room as well as the other rooms in the house, will soon be operational. What luck it was to find such interesting remnants of the past behind two layers of drywall.

New copper gutters will accentuate the roofline and keep the rain out of the Lady's eyes. Fall rains already have pounded on her roof and settled all the dust. The new Little House roofline will also have copper gutters to match the Lady's design. She is reassured as she listens in on the conversation about a two-level garage with fashionable barn doors. Windowed dormers will provide natural light and space to an area on the second floor. A large landing/porch with stairs to the lawn area will allow access to the guest room atop the garage. Outdoor entry to separate men's and ladies' bathrooms will be convenient. The third bay of the garage awaits brides and bridal attendants with dressing stations and triptych mirrors, as well as privacy from curious eyes. This will be a lovely place to prepare for a wedding or special event. The Lady can hardly contain her enthusiasm. She always loved to entertain and share herself with others.

Late afternoon brings a stirring of trees. Soon there is a gusty breeze as fluffy clouds build over the valley. The breeze becomes a strong wind, as big raindrops begin to pelt the windows, creating dirty designs on the glass. For a few minutes, rain bombards everything. Then, just as quickly the wind dies down, the clouds move out over the valley, and all is quiet again. Once again, Jerome experiences its own small weather zone, isolated from the Doppler reports. As evening approaches the temperature drops and the Lady feels a chill. Painted radiators stand at attention on the grass as if awaiting the call to battle. When Scott finishes the final floor coating, the radiators will take their rightful places in the house. Radiant heat will then create a warm, even temperature throughout the Honeymoon Cottage. The warmth will be very welcome in the early mornings. As the sun leaves the sky and beds down for the night, the thermostatically controlled radiators will heat up. Radiator heat is very even and is not subject to sudden bursts of forced air, with periods of alternating hot and cold.

Eric of Platinum Painting returns after a two-week hiatus to finish the trim work in the kitchen. The Lady awaits the application of her makeup. With her lovely new surroundings, a facial and fresh lipstick sound wonderful. The picture moldings in all the rooms please her; she will not have holes driven in her back and sides for hanging pictures.

The bath and kitchen fixtures are installed by expert plumber Robert Rose, and the Lady hopes she will have sinks and toilets soon. It has been a long time since she paid a visit to the ladies' room for a long leisurely bubble bath. The impatience that I have felt all along now transfers to the Lady as she sees the completion nearing. So close and yet so far to go. "Hurry, hurry," she says. "I want to be able to serve Thanksgiving dinner on the new table. I want to be able to smell the turkey roasting in the oven, mash the potatoes, butter the peas and carrots and slice my homemade crusty bread."

Landscapers pay the Lady a visit and walk the acreage to gain a better understanding of the scope and nature of vegetation that will grow well in Jerome. Tim and Patte from Moon Valley Nursery and Landscaping walk with my son and I as they plan the fruit orchard. Shade and accent trees will add color and dimension for effect and privacy. A hedge of rosemary will line the upper level trailing down over the 12-foot wall to grab hold between the rocks. Wildflower seeds will be thrown into crevices along with herb seeds. Sod will be placed on the upper yard, the first level and the second level.

As this area was trimmed and cleaned out, a large live oak tree was found hidden between some overgrown mesquite trees. Cleopatra Hill was once an old oak forest that was unmercifully logged for housing and firewood. What was not used was killed by sulfur emissions from nearby mining operations. What a surprise to find this wonderful old tree hidden right in front of us, still thriving.

Pathways will wind around the property with rest areas placed here and there. Rose bushes that were replanted from the front of the yard to the north and west wall are flourishing. They seem to like the shelter from the afternoon sun provided by the low rock wall.

As I leave the Lady to return to the Valley, three adult mule deer and a baby deer cross my path in front of the car. The baby stops and turns to stare at me. He winks, nods his head and scurries after his mother. Approval from wildlife is important, after all, and it seems I have it. The Lady has always been a careful steward of nature and will continue to be wise with her resources.

Nearing Completion

*L*ight leaves the sky around 5:30 each evening as the days get shorter and shorter. Sunrise peeks above the hills later each day as the winter solstice approaches. A morning sky is streaked with red, orange and yellow as the sun struggles to rise above the mountain range, and every house in town has frost on the roof. An early morning fog awaits the sun's warmth before it burns off. The last of the leaves have fallen off the apricot tree in the front of the house. Dried scrub brush and wildflower plants stand stiff and tall in the cold air. Everything has been shut down and pulled back into itself to slumber through the next few months. Deer that cross the lawn each morning find little to snack on these days. Javelina that once nestled under a mesquite tree are gone, having been exterminated by some townsfolk who were worried about their forays. The occasionally aggressive animals were seeking food too close to their homes. Men and wildlife don't always mix well.

The front lawn is now level after 162 loads of fill dirt, and the dry stack walls are all complete. The area below the walls has been cleared of all the scrub brush and will soon be ready for sod to be laid. The Lady sighs, her thoughts going back to a time when she was young and the children played hide and seek around the fruit trees in the orchard. She remembers the croquet matches on Sunday afternoons after dinner. The memories chase each other through her mind as quickly as lively kittens, of which she has also seen her share.

She looks out over and down the hillside from her front lawn and remembers the families that once lived around her perimeter. In the flat area just below her third level sat a small community called Daisy Town. There was a wonderful Hispanic community of about 1,500 people living on her border. Gone now are the old homes, and all that is left are the decrepit remnants and stone foundations. I find cracked pottery, rusty old cans. pieces of a small china doll (once the beloved companion of a little girl), clay marbles and old "funny rubber" balls. Bits and pieces of people's lives lay under layers of rubble and debris. Some have been recovered by Harry and Darin as they cleared the area; some by myself as I have walked the property. Most of the fabric that made up the quilt of life in Jerome resides now in layers of soil and in the memories of old timers still alive.

The Lady's reverie is rudely interrupted by the banging of the backhoe into the garage. Looking in the direction of the noise, she sees the demolition beginning, and her breath comes in short gasps. In a few hours, the garage will be completely gone. The next day, the old concrete slab – raised in the middle and badly cracked – is chewed up by the backhoe, and load after load is taken down beyond the third level and used as fill. Now nothing remains but bare earth. It is with mixed emotions that the Lady looks out over where the garden once was. She always wondered why the Southwestern stepchild was erected next to her elegant French country walls in the first place. She is sure that the new garage, with a $7/12$ pitch roof like her own, will be pleasing. Peering over

Phil Wright's shoulder as he and I discuss the progress and cost, she likes what she hears. The dormers upstairs and a stairway off a new landing that overlooks the Valley are very nice touches, she thinks. She anticipates greeting this new child with open arms.

The stepchild came down quickly. Heartache followed the demolition of the structure, which, despite the Lady's attachment to it, was not salvageable. No footings, small stem walls and slab riddled with large cracks throughout the cement allowed for no repair. There was no way to build a second floor and dormers above the garage for a guest room. Destruction and starting over were the only options. Still, the Lady missed her close friend and was lonely for companionship.

The 'iron maiden', (an impersonal metal storage container) that stands nearby is from another era altogether, and they have so little in common that neither spoke to the other. When the old garage was gone, the space between the two was just too far, and both realized that the iron maiden's days were numbered; she was only a "temp".

The iron maiden is a large metal container that moved back and forth across the Atlantic and Pacific oceans in large container ships. They carried no passengers and were loaded with cargo. After many, many voyages back and forth from one continent to another, they are scuffed and banged up and are replaced with new units. The used containers are then sold for use as storage units. They have large doors that provide access to the unit and lock for security and safety. They are waterproof and constructed of very heavy steel. Needing a place to store furniture and personal items during the construction of the new garage, I purchased an iron maiden, which we placed next to the old garage and filled to the hilt.

I used the container for several months, and although she and the Lady were physically close to each other, they were never close friends. Upon completion of the garage, Harry moved the container to his property to use as storage. I soon missed the extra storage room, as I needed a place to keep the garden tools, wheelbarrows and other assorted yard items. A few weeks after the original iron maiden left, a newer version was placed next to the low dry stack wall along the driveway. It fit perfectly in-between a large pine tree and the low wall on the west side of the house. With such close proximity to the Lady, it was not long before they were exchanging stories. The Lady was interested in hearing of the many exotic places the new resident has visited and the 'maiden' was eager to learn about her new surroundings. They soon became fast friends.

Eric has returned and finished painting the basement, the kitchen and the shutters, with the understanding that there will be some touchup required in the future. All the drawers and doors are now painted and ready for the pulls and knobs to be reattached. The stove and refrigerator are in place in the kitchen, ready to perform, and every bathroom has been outfitted with a toilet, sink and tub. The radiators are all in their rightful places, and the heating system is working well.

My children and I begin applying a polyurethane finish on the floor early on Thanksgiving Saturday. The first coat goes on easily, and the entire house is soon complete with the exception of the living room, which is loaded with furniture from the garage. On Sunday, sore bodies all around, we jump right in to complete the job. You would think that the second coat would go on more easily, however, it actually took longer. By 1 P.M. the second coat has been applied, and the Lady is locked up so no one will step on her floors until they are dry. The honey-colored sheen of the wood is beautiful, and the Lady smiles as she admires the hand-applied finish. Four people leave Jerome with sore backs and aching muscles that are seldom used, each knowing that a hot shower will cure most of the discomfort.

Out front, the little Bobcat scrapes layer after layer of dirt that washed off the hill so many years ago. He carries it away to fill areas by the front terrace, and another step is revealed at each door. Harry will pour stem walls for the new garage, while laying down a new walkway at the same time. A winding sort of walkway led from the parking area to the door when the Lady was young, and it will now be replicated with this new walkway.

"Be careful of my new floor," says the Lady. "Please do not come in with muddy feet. You will scratch my beautiful finish, and I will be very upset." Dirty shoes may be set on an old cotton rag rug next to the solid cherry wood door that Walter built. The door has eight small windows of old seeded glass; it is beautiful and well made. Only stocking feet are allowed in the house right now, and many pairs of shoes cover the rug. The Lady appreciates that people care about her shiny new floors.

The new handcrafted window cranks at all the windows open and close well. A few of the windows stick with excess paint, but Walter will plane them down so they all open and close easily. Every one of the doors is hung, and the swinging door leading from the butler's pantry into the dining room now boasts a beveled glass window.

Floors, walls and light fixtures were dusted and cleaned. Walls with rough plaster finish had to be vacuumed as there was so much dust and dirt clinging to them. The Lady feels cleansed to her very core, her spirits lifted and brightened with long-awaited new life.

There is still so much to do that at times it seems overwhelming. Most of the light fixtures and ceiling fans are installed. Patio lights have yet to be hooked up, and the ceiling of the deck still needs to be painted. A myriad of little odds and ends must be resolved. The Lady looks forward to the day when furniture will fill the rooms and a family will again sleep in her beds, eat at her tables and gaze out her windows over the scenic Verde Valley.

December brings frosty mornings that coat the puddles from last week's rain with an icy film. Stepping in the puddles is like shattering glass. The moisture dries up quickly as gravity pulls the water out of the mud and down the hillside. Soon, all this dirt will be covered with grass, sidewalks and steppingstones. Flowers will fill the Lady's bedding areas, and fruit and flowering trees will add accent, color and summer shade.

The Lady stops to take inventory of the past year. It seems like a lifetime ago that she first heard my voice and whispered back to me her deepest desires. This past year has gone by so quickly. Her new beautiful attire is so very different from the dilapidated wretched rags she once wore. Her new blue hat, lovely yellow dress and beautiful copper trim all complement her new paint. She hums along with the birds chirping around her head as she anticipates the adventures brought by each new day.

Footnote:
The Lady hopes to be fully furnished by Christmas so that she can host a few holiday events. The new garage should have the walls and the beginning of a roofline by the end of the year, and all must be completed by April 12, 2003, the date of the first wedding in the Honeymoon Cottage.

Button Up Your Overcoat
When the Wind Blows Free

*D*ark skies over Mingus Mountain threaten the sun that struggles to shine through between the clouds. Morning begins with frozen ground cracking beneath the feet until the sun hits and turns the surface to mud. Ice puddles, having frozen solid during the night, melt and become muddy quagmires. As the day warms up, jackets are shed. Activity around the Lady is noisy and disruptive as she slowly awakens. These cool mornings in December and early January lend themselves to late rising. Watching the sun rise over the mountains to the east is far better from a warm bed than from a chilly patio.

Harry cranks up the engine on the backhoe and is soon pushing dirt around below the big wall. A road winds along the first 12-foot supporting wall and makes a hairpin turn at the north end of the property before winding back down to the south, where it then makes a sharp turn and feathers out into the flatter part of the front yard. Here at a grove of evergreen trees, the road ends. A marriage ceremony held here and viewed from three terrace levels will ensure that every person has a good seat. Only three months until the big day. Is there enough time to get everything finished for the wedding? "One day at a time," the Lady says. "Just as with moving and settling in, when all those boxes seemed to be an insurmountable task to unpack, it all happened. It is true that the longest journey starts with the first step."

As Harry prepared the area, excavating the ground for proper new footings and stem walls, the Lady watched with renewed interest. As the cement truck backed its way down the road from the turn on Douglas, it passed the old storage facility of core samples at the corner. It lumbered on past Deans Bubolo's (the shower house for the miners) and then continued past the Kingdon House, (built by the Douglas family for the Mine Superintendent), the home just to the south of the Honeymoon Cottage. The big truck stopped at the construction forms beside her, and the Lady watched the cement truck pour a stream of concrete to fill them up. A few days later, the forms were pulled, and the cement truck again backed up to the house to pour the main slab, its incessant beeping alerting all of its arrival. After a few days of cement curing, the framers arrived to begin erecting the guesthouse. The trusses will arrive in a week or two, and there will be a flurry of activity as we rush to complete this new structure in time for the wedding.

Dave Strube, a general contractor from Sedona, has contracted to build the guesthouse. Phil, buried under prior commitments, could not complete the structure in time. Dave has stepped up, and construction moves forward. Dave brings 12 years of construction experience with him and is well qualified to complete this new addition.

The sound of metal on metal echoes across the valley. The old fencing at the edge of the property is moved around and examined by a man who has been a metal worker for years. A fence will be built across the south end of the driveway, up the west hill and down the east hill to shield the Lady from prying eyes. Security and privacy are necessary, as the Lady is clearly visible from so many areas of Jerome. She always was a private person, and although eager to share herself with invited guests and friends, she is wary and cautious of strangers who in the past have almost strangled her – once as silver light fixtures were pulled from her walls, dragging wires helplessly behind them. Her walls were injured and abused and, at times, people created hazardous situations that placed themselves and her in danger. Now, in all new finery, she is alert to any intrusion from people she does not know.

Work continues on the outside of the Little House, while inside the Lady opens cabinets in the kitchen to reveal stacks of pots and pans that, without shelves to sit on, stack up on each other. Cabinet doors do not close fully, and some cabinet doors are missing altogether. Shelves that were warped were thrown into the big green dumpster. All the drawer pulls, cabinet latches and hinges have to be pulled and cleaned. Year after year, they were painted over with a variety of colors.

David Skimin, a finish carpenter, will arrive early in January to build shelves, hang doors with new hinges, fix cabinet doors and complete closets. He will make sure all doors have knobs and that they will open and close properly. Drawers will have guides installed so they will move easily. Old wood cabinetry has its own set of rules when it comes to functioning properly and must be coaxed into submission. Old galvanized steel bins that once held grains and vegetables must be pressed back into operation carefully and tenderly or they will pull out the stops on the cabinet. Only someone with kind and gentle hands is able to persuade the old wood to respond. Bit by bit, the work is getting done, but some of these tasks seem to take forever. These jobs are not always as evident as the larger projects.

My son John spent a long weekend hanging a mirror in the dining room and assembling stainless steel shelving in the basement, putting the washer and dryer in place and completing various other odd jobs that seemed to pop up out of nowhere. The challenge of finding picture molding hooks that will hold pictures as in 1921 lies in front of us. A picture railing runs around each room, about one inch lower than the ceiling. Paintings, pictures and other items for display were wired and hung from a hook that curled around the top edge of the railing. There were no holes or nails used in plaster walls, as this would crack and break the plaster. The picture hooks could be slid along the picture railing to easily move what was hung on them. All it took was a tall ladder and a good sense of balance.

The patio under the deck was cleaned up that same long weekend. All the old wood, leftover screws, nails, old window cranks and other remnants of when the Lady was gutted are sorted through. Some are kept and some are tossed into the dumpster.

Around the foundations of the Lady, small green shoots and leaves push up through the dirt. The ivy that wound up and around the wall and windows is determined to find its place in the grand scheme of things. Decorative shutters will soon be hung next to the windows and may not be able to support the weight of the ivy. Windows that already do not close completely (part of every house in Jerome is drafty) would find themselves in conflict with plants growing in and around them.

More Chores for the Lady of the House

*H*aving a crew of strong men around is very helpful. Earlier in the month, Harry and Walter moved a Murphy bed I purchased from an antique shop into the sun room upstairs next to the master bedroom. When the bed was closed, a beautiful mirror surrounded by ornamental hand-carved wood was revealed. My son assembled the bed, which is very unique and truly beautiful. It also weighed a lot and was difficult to move. Harry and Abe Stewart, his nephew, struggle to move the Murphy bed down the stairs from the sun room (probably a nursery – next to the Master bedroom), to be set up in the maid's room. The day bed that was intended to go in the maid's room did not fit against the wall space – the Murphy bed did. What once was a great feat to move upstairs (solid oak and heavy metal bed springs) became just as difficult to move back downstairs. One step at a time, Harry and Abe navigate around the turn on the stairway to reach the landing. They then negotiate another flight of stairs to the entry. The Lady turns her head as she hears groaning and grumbling from the two men as they strain under the weight of this old bed. "Isn't it just like a woman to change her mind all the time?" they laugh. They wind around the corner through the kitchen, into the hall and finally into the small maid's room. The other half of the bed soon follows. Pieces are assembled, and, just as we thought, the bed is a perfect fit. The Lady just smiles as they set the bed down and take a deep breath.

The day bed sits against the west wall in the sun room; the trundle underneath will provide extra sleeping room for guests. Harry and Abe collapse on the steps and sit for a few minutes to catch their breath. I wonder how in the world people years ago managed to move those heavy Murphy beds (or parlor beds, as they were called). I'll just bet they set them up and never moved them again in their lifetime.

Danny Rowley, from Old Town Electric, installed all the outside lights that now cast a soft glow around the entrance. On the patio, small copper lights provide a dark area with good lighting. The lamps look as though they have always been there and fit in well with their copper finish and early 20th century design. Light kits have been affixed to the fans, and each room now has a main ceiling light in addition to small wall lights. Only the patio ceiling fans have yet to be installed.

In the basement, the pressure release valve on the hot water heater continues to give us grief. A plumber from Cornville is called in to fix the problem, as Robert Rose, our primary plumber, is on vacation in Florida. The small amount of water on the floor must be removed quickly or moisture will undermine and delaminate the slate. A small drainage line will be installed to keep the water off the floor. The plumber will also fix a leaking valve on the small maid's room shower at the tub. The Lady shakes her head from side to side as she sees all these small annoyances that seem to take so much time to fix. It just goes with the territory, she surmises. She knows I will see to it that everything is re-solved satisfactorily because my "dog-gone German work ethic that says you do it right or not at all" prevails in my life consistently. There will be no "patch-up" jobs for the Lady now; everything will be done right and proper.

A New Friend for the Lady

$\mathcal{L}$ingering memories wander in and out of the Lady's consciousness in her efforts to come to grips with the recent changes taking place around her. Only a short time ago, her companion of the past five years, the Santa Fe style garage, was gone in but a few short hours. The roof was removed and the walls knocked down and carried away, the slab flooring lifted by the backhoe and hauled away piece by piece, taken to an area where it was used as fill and covered with dump loads of dirt. The Lady felt sad as her friend was taken down. An acute sense of loneliness followed. Though they had little in common, he did provide company. Having no close neighbors meant long hours alone. She so looked forward to the weekends when I would bring up my two dogs, Copper and Lucky. She loved having her floors vacuumed and then mopped with Murphy's Oil soap massaging the wood and leaving a shiny clean floor. Soon, the grass sod would be laid, and there would be little dust and dirt dragged in on the bottom of shoes. Neither would the dogs track in mud and dirt.

The stillness of the weekdays is replaced on the weekends by the two dogs chasing each other across the front yard. Lucky picks up a stuffed dog toy from the basket where they are kept and drops it on the dirt. Copper picks up the toy and runs across the yard, and Lucky gives chase. My whistle beckons them back into the house at dusk. The smell of bacon in the morning and supper in the evening evokes memories of the years when the house was filled with family and fun.

Now in my midyears, I enjoy the quiet companionship of the Lady as approaching dusk pushes the sun behind Mingus Mountain. I curl up on the sofa with a book and feel the Lady snuggle around me. A view from the dining room window reveals twinkling flickers in Cottonwood and Clarkdale as lights click on for evening illumination. Everyone and everything hunkers down for the night as the temperature drops to the near-freezing mark.

Around 6:30 A.M., the sky to the east begins to lighten and is soon glowing red over the mountains. By 7 A.M., the sky is pink and yellow, each cloud etched in color. A large ball of bright yellow appears, and the sky turns daybreak blue.

Hustle and bustle greet the Lady as the framers arrive with their trailer, a generator for their nail guns in tow. The wood was dropped off several days ago, and the foundation, stem walls, footings and slab were poured then as well. We await the next step. By early afternoon, the basic outline of the new garage is visible and begins to take shape. By late afternoon, the shape of the Little House is there for the Lady to admire. Within a few days, the second floor is up, the roof is on and dormers peer out from the second floor. The Little House opens its eyes for the first time and is startled to see the Lady standing just to the north. The Little House smiles at the Lady, and she knows they will be good friends. She welcomes the companionship, and the Little House, too, is happy to have a friend.

Ed and Sally Gonzalez buzz around like busy bees stringing all the electric wiring throughout the house. Danny Rowley, who rewired the Lady, clues the Gonzalez team in on all the odd intricacies of what has gone on before. Ceiling fans, special lighting and the heating and cooling systems all need custom wiring. Mark Wilcox, the plumber from Cornville, is plumbing the Little House and is working closely with general contractor David Strube. It won't be long before Richard Peek arrives to put blue shingles on the roof that match the blue on the Lady.

A Gannon (a large machine with a bucket in front, teeth in the back and a scraper) grumbles and rumbles up the winding road into Jerome, pulling over periodically to let less cumbersome vehicles pass. At 15 miles an hour, the trek up the hill takes a good half hour. Bouncing down the dirt road to the house, Robert Rose, now back from vacation, arrives. He pulls up next to the house, and the Gannon lumbers to a halt. As soon as the engine is turned off, the grumbling stops, and for a minute or two, the silence is deafening. This large bulldozer will rake and move and then smooth out the earth. All this activity is preparation of the soil for the sod that will arrive soon.

First, the area below the Lady must be cleared of everything that has accumulated over the last 80 years. My son John, Darin (well known for building our 12-foot dry stack retaining wall) and Leo Shakespeare, a townie and newcomer to the Lady but a longtime resident of Jerome, begin the job. They remove the useless water heaters, assorted dead branches, remnants of cleared trees and just plain old junk from the lower levels. Then John, now operating the big Gannon, begins the grading. He contours the terraces below the rock walls, leveling and smoothing as he goes. As he fills the bucket with dirt and moves it here and there, it soon becomes evident how the terraces will wind down to the flat place by the trees. The winding road is angled, and wildflower seed will be sown in areas where there is no grass. Trees, shrubs and other plants like roses, oleanders, rosemary and other herbs will be planted and encouraged to grow. With the wonderful morning sun and the perfectly shaded afternoons, one would be hard pressed to find a better growing environment. Rose bushes against the rock wall to the north of the Lady love their new location. New bare-root roses will soon join these older bushes, and all are expected to do well.

Next week, John and a crew will lay the PVC pipe for the watering system. Gathering and assembling all the items needed proved to be quite the challenge. Many of the pipes were too long and had to be bent and curved to fit into the old U-Haul truck John purchased to transport stuff between his vineyard in Wilcox and Jerome. This big white box on a pickup frame uses diesel. We like to refer to the vehicle as "Urban Oil Rocket." In the center of the box sit two pallets of 16 × 16 travertine for the patio and entryways. All around are lengths of PVC, black tubing, tools to cut PVC, glue and assorted paraphernalia for the job. Travertine is very heavy, but Urban can handle the job. "Throw more pallets on my back!" he growls. "I'm ready."

Rain, Rain and More Rain: Will It Ever Stop?

*W*ater runs ferociously down the hill behind the Lady, taking out part of the west dry stack wall. She shudders in fear as she recalls the spring of '67, when heavy melting snow and early rains took out the little garage that sat behind her. The top rocks fall into the mud, followed soon after by the larger rocks, which just sort of slide out of place, opening the floodgates. Mud, plant material and small rocks now pour into and through the opening in the wall, and rivulets of rainwater join forces with runoff from the Lady's roof. Ground made loose from last week's grading easily gives in to the merciless torrent of rushing water. Small rivulets quickly turn into deep, wide furrows. The water moves along the sidewalk, turns the corner between the Lady and the little garage and bolts across the south lawn toward the big wall. Accelerating to the edge, it streams over the rocks as a rushing waterfall. Crashing into the second terrace, it brandishes new strength, cutting through the soft earth and racing down the hill onto the third terrace, all the while pushing small rocks out of its way. Halfway down the hill, the flow collects in a low spot and quickly becomes a small pond. The rain continues for hours, and everything is mired down in mud. Walking across the yard the next day, shoes gather extra pounds of mud that add inches to one's height. The Lady dreads days like this as she becomes the recipient of all the debris from such heavy-laden shoes. She sighs and settles into the inevitable. "Indeed, I've been through much worse," she laments.

Days after the three-and-a-half inches of rain Jerome received, the ground is still seeping water into the lower levels of the yard. Lower temperatures in the morning have workers walking on frozen mud that fills the ruts cut by the water. As the day warms, the mud melts and becomes soft and sticky. Machinery has trouble trenching through the wet earth. A few days of sun and the ground is drier, except on the lower levels. The pond begins to evaporate. A trencher cuts into the ground and soon there are spaghetti lines of PVC lacing the terraces. The air smells of plastic and glue as fittings are attached to pipe and joints connect section after section of the sprinkler system. The Lady has never seen anything like this before. In the past, she relied on nature to keep her flowers and plants watered. She is intrigued by the complexity of this new system and is anxious to see how it all works.

The Little House, just barely awakening to these goings-on, looks at the activity with awe and concern. His trim work, freshly painted prior to the rain, has blistered and peeled. The new oil paint did not have time to dry prior to the rainfall. Blisters rip open from the weight of the water, and he knows that scraping and repainting await him in drier days. Inside and upstairs, Mark Wilcox installs the on-demand hot water heater, the water lines and the sink and shower connections. Extra spigots are installed outside, along with a shower to rinse off garden dirt.

Over the weekend, I bring up some plants that now sit along the east wall. The contrast of the greenery against the gray rock is lovely. The Lady has been without vegetation for so long that seeing the blue flowers on the rosemary bushes brings tears to her eyes. She did not realize she missed the greenery so much. Geraniums with big fluffy clusters of red flowers line the wall, and additional herbs, shrubs and perennials await planting. The Urban Oil Rocket has been loaded with all the newly purchased vegetation to make the long haul up the hill from the Phoenix area. Urban, even with all his grumbling, has proven to be a hard, dependable worker that just "keeps on truckin".

Copper trim now lines the two brick chimneys on the Lady's roof and runs down the furrows on the roof and along the trim board. Now bright and shiny, the copper will soon turn green and brown as it oxidizes and create a good break of color between the blue roof and the yellow house. One old section of original copper roofing will be cleaned and brightened up to match the new trim.

Outside on the patio under the deck, Victor Senne, the tile setter, and his crew lay the blue and yellow-veined travertine. A sidewalk will be added leading from the patio to the stairs of the Little House and also from the sidewalk in front of the house to the garage. Sod is ordered and will soon be laid on top of tons of topsoil. Dormant Bermuda grass that has been over-seeded with rye should do very well in Jerome's high desert climate. The grass will run all across the top terrace, along the 12-foot wall on the second level and wind on down to the third level. A small clearing under our large oak tree will have a bench and a flowerbed. The third level will serve as a wedding staging area, with trees curving gracefully around a flat grassy landing, where the bride and groom will join as husband and wife. Guests of the happy couple will have a full view of the ceremony and a spectacular view of the entire Verde Valley.

Back inside, preparations are made for the Lady's window coverings to be installed. Packages are piled throughout the dining room and the living room, filled with items for the wedding. Several metal arches will be decorated with white ribbons and flowers to frame the bride and groom as they exchange their vows.

Although the weather dried up for a few days, a new storm moves in, and Jerome's own little weather system again steps up to the plate. The town of Cottonwood, only four miles below us, basks in crisp sunshine as snow falls on Jerome. Intermittent days of rain and sun in the valley below mean hail, heavy rain and snow up the hill where the big J is covered with fluffy white stuff. (Many towns and cities have a letter – the first of their name – on a hillside which identifies them. They are visible to aircraft flying overhead and at night are illuminated by solar lights.)

By now, the ground is so wet that walking across the yard adds, once again, pounds of mud to our shoes. Each step is an effort, and we feel like astronauts walking on the moon. The dogs track in mud, the workers track in mud, and I track in mud! The Lady grins and bears it all as she waits for the sunny and dry days ahead. After more than a week of rain, the snow comes down hard on Saturday night. Early Sunday morning, the rising sun glistens on a crystalline layer of icy snow. The apricot tree sheds its snowy mantle as the rays of the sun melt the ice. Even the garden tractor is covered with snow. By 11 A.M., the sunshine has melted the snow into another muddy mess, and the resulting furrows in the topsoil are eight inches deep. Muddy water quickly seeps into our shoes and stains our white socks. Through the slippery mud, Leo, Darin and I move plants and shrubs into position to be placed in the soft ground.

On Sunday afternoon, the sun warms the day and plants are placed around the walls.

Throughout Monday morning, the planting continues, and we discover that the truckload of plants Urban hauled up from the valley is not enough to cover the bedding area. More vegetation is needed. Rosemary will form a border along the 12-foot wall. Indian hawthorn, a very dark green leafed shrub with pink flowers, will line the second wall. Lavender wraps around the corners of the walls, and bougainvillea plants stand in a row, waiting to climb over the small rock area at the north end of the yard and saunter up the hillside. Already, this little bit of color changes the entire look of the Lady.

Rain is again forecast for Wednesday, but it should be a minor storm, and the gardens will welcome the sprinkling. The moisture will help germinate the countless wildflower seeds that Leo and I spread on Sunday afternoon. A changing sky, one moment filled with bright colors and clouds and the next streamers of sunshine, mesmerizes the gardeners as they gaze across the valley. The snow-covered San Francisco Peaks (north of Flagstaff and visible from the front yard of the Lady) and snowy frosting of Sedona's red rocks shows Mother Nature at her finest. For a few minutes, the mud is forgotten.

Shingles lie atop felt on the roof of the Little House, awaiting drier days for installation. Stucco follows the roofing shingles, and interior drywall is close behind. Time is of the essence now as the happy day quickly approaches. Like a puzzle, each piece of this construction project is coming together. The Lady holds her breath now to see if all the pieces will connect in time.

On a Roll Fraught
with Challenges

March 26, 2003

Time has departed. The Lady is agitated, anxious and nervous all at the same time. The Little House is not complete, the roof half-done and the stucco not yet applied. Inside, drywall awaits texturing. So much to do and so little time. The rains of last month backed everything up about three weeks, but we can't delay the wedding! Drywall could not be hung until the electrical and plumbing work was completed. Insulation could not be installed until it passed inspection by the county. Painting can't take place until the roof is done, and the painting that was done on the exterior was ruined by the rain and must be reapplied.

Disappointment burdens the Lady and covers the Little House like a shroud. Richard Peek had done such a good job on the Lady's blue bonnet that I wanted to engage him to complete the Little House as well. Unfortunately, he was unavailable. The warm sunny days, perfect for roofing, turned cold and rainy and soon the felt, laid on the roof to cushion the shingles, was soaking wet. Now it is too dangerous to work on the roof. Dave, our general contractor, brought in some roofers from Flagstaff to finish the job, but the shingles are so poorly applied that they must be ripped off from a large section of the roof. Dave and I are next to frantic. The roof has held up progress on everything else.

Inside the Lady, I sweep, vacuum and wash all the floors. The whole house smells like Murphy's Oil Soap. A large black rug with a rooster design arrives and is laid under the dining room table. Irme Obermeier, owner of Windows by Design, installs all the window treatments, and the Lady looks finished with her lovely window coverings. Sheer curtains in the bedrooms allow vision outside while preserving privacy within. The Lady envisions an open window, a soft breeze and the sheer curtains gently swaying as she breathes in the cool, clean air.

Her reverie is quickly broken as she feels the wind blow across her head. Looking up, she sees dark clouds moving in and begins to worry over another storm and more mud and mess. The rain begins softly and gently, and the moisture on her face feels wonderfully cool. Before long, however, the yard and the driveway are mushy and muddy again. She hikes up her petticoats and tiptoes across the yard. The quickening mud holds onto her shoes and pulls at them as she steps hastily across the front yard. The Little House suffers again as rain pounds on his uncovered backside. Large sheets of heavy black plastic have been laid over the felt, but the strong winds quickly blow it off and it skitters across the yard, catching on a forming nail that Harry has driven into the ground. Empty pop cans left behind by the workers roll across the yard. Plants and shrubs bend and bow to the wind. A wicked dance of greenery ensues at the edge of the rock wall. Roots of rosemary and rose bushes hold fast to the ground as the wind attempts to pull them loose.

Black clouds surround Jerome, and the higher elevations are soon dusted again with snow. The lower-lying town stays clear of the snow as the temperature hovers just above the point needed to freeze the pelting rain. Off and on again hail pounds the workers and stings their faces as little pellets of ice quickly melt on warm skin. Everything is wet again, and the muddy driveway is rutted from our vehicles. All the grading will have to be done again. "Oh, Jerome!" moans the Lady in despair. "Can't your weather cooperate?"

A few weeks prior to the wedding, the sod arrives.on two large semi-flatbed trucks loaded with 35,000 square feet of grass. Rain pounds the workers as they unload the pallets of sod. Drenched, the workers move the rolls of sod, like small throw rugs, to the areas of the upper yard where they are unrolled and placed neatly one against the other. Raincoats afford the workers welcome protection against the relentless moisture. Afternoon arrives too quickly, and the workday is done. With three more layers of ground to cover and rain still falling, the landscapers leave with a promise to return in a few days when the ground is dried out. They will run a small tractor up and down the levels to haul the sod instead of having to carry it by hand. A few more days and the entire area is covered in green grass – an instant lawn.

By the end of the week, sunshine has returned, and the upper lawn is green, full and beautiful. The dogs, seldom able to enjoy grass, run and cavort and roll on the green lawn. What a treat for them! Dogs sure have a lot of fun, the Lady thinks, and have not a care in the world. A dog's life seems like a good thing.

The extra sod not used on the Lady is taken up to town and heaped in Middle Park. Before long, the townsfolk get word and begin taking rolls home to create their own green grassy areas.

Windows are set by John as drywallers arrive, and Dave hangs the doors to close up the house. Quickly, the drywallers tape and texture the inside. The Little House giggles as its walls are textured. The Lady finds joy and amusement in having a youngster on the property. A crew arrives to stucco the exterior, and the next day, the Little House is textured to match the Lady. With the Little House finally beginning to take shape, cement forms are laid for the sidewalk and a small patio that will lie beneath the steps being built to the second floor. A cement apron lying along the edge of the garage doors will keep gravel from coming into the garage. Soon, the garage doors will be placed and gravel will arrive for the driveway after it is re-graded.

What a busy few weeks! I call the bride. Her wedding dress has arrived…but it's the wrong dress! Somehow the wrong style and wrong size was sent to the shop from the dress maker. Calmly, the bride informs the manager of the shop that there is not time to re-order and she wants to select another in-stock dress for the same price as her custom dress. He agrees, and she picks out another dress. As luck would have it, the bride likes the new dress even better than the previously ordered one. Fate is at work again in Jerome, and the saga continues.

So much rain had fallen, and although it delayed the laying of the sod, the extra water mess in the driveway has nourished each plant that was placed along the edges of the wall on all four levels. Jasmine blooms profusely, roses bud out, and ranunculuses explode in color. African daisies in the front of the house turn their purple faces toward the afternoon sun. Pink mallows with long graceful stems, small green leaves and dainty blossoms run along certain areas of the walls. Victor finishes the front step, and the Lady beams at her appearance. The travertine, with its hint of yellow and rusty veins, blends perfectly with the coloring of the house.

Extra cement from prior pourings created opportunities. Harry built wooden forms with metal ceiling tiles that he then filled with the extra cement to create unique pavers. These pavers now lead around the front of the house and between the Lady and the Little House. Even with all of the confusion, delay and pain of getting where she is today, all's well that ends well. From the front yard, the Lady looks out over the Verde Valley with its ever-changing colors. Almost all of our plans have come together so beautifully, and the Lady is anxious to welcome guests and loved ones in such a picture-perfect setting.

Something Old, Something New, Something Borrowed, Something Blue

Spring has teased and tempted Jerome for the past month, simultaneously bringing us warm days and freezing nights. Snow in the morning is quickly melted by mid-morning. Short sleeves during the day evolve into warm jackets in the evening. Growing things send thin green stems up through the soil, and soon, small plants are sprouting up in dry soil, in between rocks and anywhere else they can grab hold. They produce small pink blossoms that open into beautiful white flowers that resemble wild roses. Overnight, it seems, the weeds have also taken hold, and there is a green carpet of foxtail, burrs and other annoying sticky plant life to contend with. Ladybugs proliferate, and pesky gnats are everywhere. In mid-afternoon, like clockwork, the wind picks up, and the sprinklers waft mist great distances from where the water is meant to go.

Lucky runs across the lawn and takes the turn to the lower grassy area with Copper in hot pursuit. He carries a box of Ritz crackers in his mouth that he has snagged from the neighbors' open garbage can. His sharp nose picks up that there are still a few crackers left in the box. Both dogs relish the grass and roll and roll on it until they wear themselves out. A short nap in the shade revives them, and they jump up to play again.

The Lady looks out at her yard with pride and admiration. Thinking back to the condition she was in just one year ago, it is remarkable that today she wears such beautiful finery. Looking around, she sees the hustle and bustle of many people setting up tables, decorating flower carts, unfolding chairs, lacing gauze through the apricot tree and preparing for the big day. Bright-colored poppies sit in antique iron baskets and containers, and white bows adorn each chair. Ivy winds its way around the flower carts that will be used as serving stations for the food and beverages.

The caterer and his crew are busy in the kitchen preparing delicacies for the wedding guests. The brisk fresh air heightens everyone's appetite as they wait for the ceremony to begin. A scent of roses and sweet alyssum is carried on the breeze. A string quartet awaits the completion of the ceremony to serenade the wedding party. The harpsichord player and violinist begin playing, and the crowd is hushed as the ring bearer and the flower girl begin their walk down the third level of lawn toward the minister.

LuJett McCullough, from the Haven Methodist Church in Jerome, has just asked that everyone be seated so she can begin the ceremony. One by one, the bridesmaids in bright pink dresses follow each other down the aisle on the arms of the groomsmen. Soon, they are all in place on each side of LuJett, and as the guests stand, the soon-to-be Mrs. Jason Francisco Miller glides across the lawn on her father's arm. A glowing bride all dressed in white soon stands next to her man who has been waiting patiently at the decorated arch with the minister. The vows are exchanged after a short reading by the bride's older sister, Melanie, and months and months of planning culminate in a newly married couple.

Guests erupt into applause as two happy young people begin a life filled with promise and opportunity. There are tears, smiles and congratulations for the couple. Two families are united and expanded as the fabric of love between two people becomes a quilt of new relationships. All through the ceremony, the backdrop of the Verde Valley frames the wedding party in an ever-changing array of shapes and colors courtesy of Mother Nature.

The afternoon follows a familiar pattern as family and guests eat, smile for photos and move from table to table, renewing old friendships and establishing new ones. Stories are exchanged, and a festive mood permeates the celebration. The sun slips behind Mingus Mountain, and the day cools. Sweaters drape over bare shoulders, and men don jackets. The cake is cut and enjoyed, and the young people head up to town to enjoy a DJ at Paul and Jerry's Saloon. So very quickly, the day ends as the young couple prepares for their life ahead.

The Lady enjoys her restored status as the Jewel of Jerome as friends of the two families admire her new attire. The joy of children laughing and running up and down her stairs tickles her fancy. A feeling of endearment is extended to all who come through her door. She shares herself genuinely and unabashedly with no sign of vanity or haughtiness, exuding only warmth and welcome to all. Next door, the Little House sits still and sad. Only half completed, he feels somewhat left out of the festivities. The next few months will be dedicated solely to finishing this guesthouse and three-bay garage, but he is impatient awaiting his turn.

As the afternoon winds die down, guests say goodbye

to the Lady, catching a shuttle back up to town where their cars are parked. The mood is gay and heady.

The weather is cool but sunny for Sunday morning's wedding brunch. Gifts are opened after the buffet, and soon the crowd is gone. A stillness settles into a lazy day that slides into evening with ease. Lights go on in the valley below, and the moon lights the yard with an iridescent glow as the happy couple and all the guests leave the Lady and I alone to rest and recuperate.

Curiosity and Good Walking Shoes

*O*n the morning of one of these spring days, choosing to ignore the afternoon heat, the people suddenly came in droves. Leaf peepers, green thumbs and "dirt-under-the-fingernails" lovers of all things growing. The first ever garden tour of Jerome was a rousing success. Behind the rock walls, down the garden paths, under the sliding cement stairways, up the tilted steps and through the old iron gates they came. They plodded along, sniffing and smelling, touching and oohing and aahing over the many varieties of flowers and shrubs, trees and plants.

Most everything grows well at this altitude and moderate climate. A few plants, like bougainvillea, flourish in the heat of summer but die a quick death in the cooler months. Even their deep roots are unable to withstand the lower winter temperatures.

The visitors for the garden tour were given a peek into the backyards of usually private Jerome residences. This is the real Jerome, a look at the life of those who call Jerome home day after day. We live pretty much like the rest of the world, and the "garden trippers" were delighted with what they saw.

Many of the tour hosts gave small snips of plants, iris rhizomes, volunteer trees and flowers to the folks on the tour. I suppose these folks deserve some kind of reward for walking up and down and around all the streets of Jerome. The proceeds of the tour will benefit the town with a new park bench or other needed items. The residents of Jerome who opened their yards and gardens to the curious public were surprised and happy at the many positive comments from the visitors.

The Lady was saddened that she was not invited to partake in the tour. The distance from the heart of town down to Lower Bell Road was just a bit too far for many of the visitors to walk. Perhaps she will be asked to participate next year.

The Lady's Public Debut

*T*hursday evening, May 15, 60-plus volunteers tour five renovated houses that are to be a part of the upcoming Jerome Historic House Tour. Late in the afternoon, volunteers gather at the Jerome Town Hall and caravan to each house included in the tour. After this private historic tour, all gather with the Lady at the Honeymoon Cottage for a buffet supper and the chance to relax and chat. The Lady is the last home on the tour this year.

This very night, as supper is completed and volunteers mingle outside on the lawn, the solar eclipse begins. From the Lady's deck and upper lawn, the view of the eclipse is incredible. As the bright moon slowly disappears into the dark sky, one sliver at a time, the night takes on an eerie mood. Many people, all conversing at the same time, simultaneously stop. The Lady gasps as a hush falls over the group, each of us witnessing the astrological wonder of what was to earlier peoples a great mystery. Now easily explained by modern science, the effect is no less spectacular.

During the next two days, a thousand-plus people walk through the Lady's rooms as she graciously extends her welcome to all. She relishes the attention and admiration from people who attend the 38th Annual Jerome Historic Home Tour. She giggles at Carrie, my daughter, wearing an old wedding dress she retrieved from Goodwill. Carrie welcomes visitors at the door, inviting them in to meet historical interpreters dressed in 1920s attire.

Dorothy Miller, a longtime resident, charmed everyone with her stories of "many years ago" Jerome. Dorothy and her husband rebuilt the old Gibson Market, turning the condemned building into an antique and secondhand store with living quarters above. The Market was part of the home tour in 2002. I volunteered as a docent for Dorothy then, and she now repays the favor. A warm, sunny weekend greeted all the tour attendees who finished up at Spook Hall for lemonade and cookies, the end to a perfect back-to-the-'20s experience.

An Early Morning Tragedy

*M*ay fades off the calendar with a tragedy that brings home how very precarious and fragile our lives really are. Morning coffee is interrupted by a loud noise, much like a door being slammed shut by a gust of wind. The dogs begin barking. Soon they are running across the front lawn with me in hot pursuit. We are racing toward a plume of smoke rising from the gully below the north end of the yard.

Across the canyon to the east, Bert Doss sits on her deck enjoying an early morning coffee. Bert is a member of the Jerome Volunteer Fire Department. She watches as a small homemade plane makes dips and dives in and out of the canyons around Jerome. The ominous sound of the engine stalling precedes the plane crashing at the bottom of the rock tailings that border the Lady's yard. Bert calls for help and quickly drives over to my home. She follows the dogs and I as we attempt to move close to the crash scene.

In a few minutes, two Jerome Fire Department trucks pull into the driveway. A few of the volunteer firefighters quickly don yellow protective suits, and before long they are at the site of the crash. The rocky location makes accessibility very difficult, and fire extinguishers and rescue gear must be backpacked in.

The volunteers hike back up to the Lady with sad news. Unfortunately, there are no survivors. Both the pilot and passenger were killed in the crash.

The EMTs from the Jerome Volunteer Fire Department pull on hazmat suits and begin the trip down to the crash site to retrieve the bodies. The trip down is hazardous, as a trail must be cut out of the underbrush to reach the site. An old road is discovered that makes the trip somewhat easier but no less sad. The victims were laid on the back seat of a quad that the fire department borrowed from town. There were no stretchers, and the Jerome Fire Department did not have body bags, so I gave them two new blankets from my linen closet in which they wrapped the bodies and brought them up to the hearse waiting in the driveway. The enormity and severity of this task is evident upon the faces of the EMTs and in the countenance of Mayor Jay Kinsella, who drives the quad up and down this rough trail to where the plane crashed.

Each volunteer firefighter and EMT is to be commended for their dedication and professionalism. On a moment's notice, they drop whatever they are doing and rush to the aid of their fellow man. Wearing heavy fire-protective gear and hazmat suits in 95-degree weather is difficult. Often without proper footwear or equipment, they scramble over rough terrain to rescue hikers, fight fires and protect property at all times of the night and day. They take their positions very seriously and conduct all of their training on their own time and at their own expense. I am impressed at the service and commitment this small-town volunteer group gives to the community.

Later in the day, several firemen came by my home to check on me and make sure that I was doing OK. This sad accident became very personal to each of them and to me, because of the proximity of the crash site to the Honeymoon Cottage. The Lady grieves also. She sees the pain and sorrow the firemen are experiencing. She knows that I, having experienced the recent death of my son and my husband, understand the sadness the families of the pilot and passenger will feel.

I walk down to the crash site the next day. A soft rain begins to fall as the dogs and I wind around the huge boulders, clumps of blooming cactus and century plants. The plane lies strewn over the bottom of an enormous mountain of leftover tailings from the mines. The area is quiet now. The rescue and recovery activities have ceased. In days to come, the FAA will send specialists to examine the site and determine the cause of the crash. There are a few cows grazing on a nearby hill, and a feeling of peace and serenity has replaced the destructive intensity of yesterday. How very fast and unexpectedly events occur that can change our lives and the lives of those around us forever.

Summer Doldrums, a.k.a
The Dog Days of Summer

*T*he warm days flowed into cool, pleasant evenings in early June. The briskness of the morning held into mid-afternoon, and a late-day breeze quelled any lingering heat. July rode into summer on a fire-breathing wind. Early day begged for the cool to remain, but there was no keeping the determined high temperatures away. Swamp coolers and air conditioners were switched on, and the residents of Jerome sought out the shady, cool places in their yards, armed with lemonade and iced tea.

Many residents sit under paradise trees. Though they are a joy to behold, it is quite a challenge to live with them. Their seeds were strewn from airplanes many years ago to help reforest the barren hillsides. Whatever timber the copper mines and ore smelters used to process the copper denuded the area of all vegetation. Paradise trees were a quick fix. However, as with most quick fixes, there is a downside. The trees seed themselves, as they drop their blossom clusters. They also send new seedlings up from the roots of older trees, and these darn trees grow just about anywhere they want to. Sprouts can be seen peeking out of solid rock walls and out the edges of building foundations. They are also extremely difficult to eliminate. Jerome has developed a love-hate affair with these prolific shade trees over the years.

At the Honeymoon Cottage, the days are lazy and not very productive. The sprinkling system is still undergoing refinement and tweaking at one station or another. Most of the grass is struggling, as its young roots are not yet deep enough and surface water is quickly evaporated. The Lady knows that by next year the growing landscape will all have a better footing and root system. It will then be easier for the gardens and sod to withstand the summer dryness. Most of the flowering plants have hung on, even through the weeks when there was no water due to a break in the irrigation system.

The roses, in all their flowering glory, love both the morning sun and the shade in the afternoon. Each bush seems to try to outdo the others in color and size of bloom. The rosemary is filling out and soon will provide a hedge along the upper wall. It will be a good thing to have a barrier there, as that 12-foot drop to the second terrace is a big step.

The small grapevines planted along the walls are unfurling their leaves, and tendrils are winding up through the rocks, grabbing hold wherever they can. Most of these vines are table grapes and will provide food for the birds. These days, our feathered friends are feasting on the apricot tree that stands in the front yard, its bent branches filled with the most delectable pink-yellow fruit. Easy to eat, with only a small pit that lets loose quickly, the sweet apricot pulp is a wonderful and irresistible treat from Mother Nature. Even the dogs find the fallen fruit palatable. This old tree is the only one left from the original orchard that once grew around the Lady. Surrounding the old tree are young cherry, apple, Chinese pear, nectarine and plum trees. Directions on how to survive wet years, dry years and near drought are passed on from the old tree to these young upstarts.

Jingling bells cause the Lady to listen closely, and she wonders what is coming down the road. Down the rocky narrow back road from town trot two horses pulling a surrey with fringe on top. Horse and buggy rides delight visitors to Jerome and carry them to seldom seen places off the beaten path. Children and elders alike gravitate to this turn-of-the-century mode of transportation, and the owner/driver, Bob Peterson, a true to life old cowboy, has a reputation for story telling, which makes the ride even more fun. The slower pace gives all an opportunity to take in the many points of interest. The Lady listens as Bob tells his passengers all about her.

These are the times when everything slows down. Folks don't move as fast in the heat. Most everyone takes the time in the afternoon to stop and sip some tea or linger over lunch. Vacations are planned to cooler climates and chores put off till the weather cools. Most of the wild grasses and flowers that surround the Lady are now dormant. Wild wheat waves from an amber field of grain that covers the lower part of the property. Many plants now spew forth their seeds at the least hint of a breeze that will carry their progeny to a new place to grow in the spring.

Old Fashioned Fourth of July

*F*ourth of July celebrations are held in every city and town across America, and Jerome is no exception. A potluck dinner in Middle Park and a dance in the evening at Spook Hall to benefit the volunteer fire department are all part of being a "Jeromie" and an American. Young and old alike sport the colors of the USA, the red, white and blue melding into a quilt of patriotism. We who live in this wonderful country are truly blessed, and picnics, barbecues and parties are a great way to celebrate our diversity and our unity.

Hot dogs, hamburgers and apple pie bring out good old American traditions in all of us. The Fourth of July town picnic in Jerome looked like a Norman Rockwell painting. As Mayor Kinsella flipped the burgers and hot dogs, the grill wafted smoke upward from Middle Park, and a table laden with salads, fruit, special dishes and condiments lured town residents back again and again to load up plates of food. Every half hour or so, new arrivals set dishes of food on the table, which meant additional trips for a taste of the new fare.

The shade of the park and the cool breeze kept everyone comfortable, as the temperature is typically about 15 degrees lower than Phoenix. Stories were swapped, tales were told, friendships were renewed and new folks introduced to the locals. A small group of musicians played while children danced and sang along. A few lucky dogs even made snacks of dropped food.

The old Jerome fire engine delighted young children, who scrambled up and down and all over the old truck. No longer carrying firefighters to the scene of an emergency, the old girl now just sits as a tourist attraction in downtown Jerome, being brought out for town functions. Today the truck gives the youngsters rides around town, their squeals letting everyone know how much fun they are having.

The Jerome town picnic is reminiscent of yesteryear and is a step back in time to a slower pace. The day ends as dusk encroaches, and down in the Verde Valley the fireworks in Cottonwood are lighting up the nighttime sky.

Monsoons Move In

$\mathcal{I}$t is that time of year again when late summer delineates itself from the other seasons with hot, stagnant days that become almost unbearable in the afternoon. The air is oppressive and heavy, and energy levels reach new lows. The dogs snooze on the grass next to the garage. I sit with my visitors on the swing under the deck and sip cool drinks. At about three in the afternoon, the breeze slips quietly between the two buildings and brushes against hot moist skin to cool everyone down. Later in the day, as the sun begins its descent behind Cleopatra Hill, the breeze picks up and becomes robust, blowing needles from the dry pine trees all over the yard. Occasionally, a pine cone will fall, and the dogs race over to see what it is. The lilac bushes, the roses and even the drought-resistant rosemary droop and sag from the dry heat. The water given in the morning has all but evaporated by late afternoon. At this time of year, every living thing struggles to stay alive until the monsoons hit.

Lightning and heavy black clouds fold into each other as the sky darkens and threatens rain. Oftentimes, hail precedes the moisture. Sometimes the threat never materializes and the very few drops that fall just make the heat all the more oppressive.

The tall pines are suffering a slow death from the bark beetle that, like the termite, relishes this dry wood. In good times, the trees are able to repel the beetle by using their sap to push the insect out. When times are dry, however, and the drought goes on year after year, the trees pull what little moisture they have into themselves. The sap moves toward the middle of the tree as they try to outlive the drought, and the beetle has easy access to the weakened tree. Two large ponderosa pines on the west side of the Lady's landscape have already died, while several others are struggling. Scotty Nesselrode, long time townie and a gardner, cares about these giant trees. He and I water them by sprinkling them high up on the trunk and letting the water trickle down. The beetles do not like the moisture, and the hope is that the water will repel them. Scotty comes to the Lady each and every day to water his big trees. All over Mingus Mountain are large swaths of brown dead trees. Sadness fills the eyes of the Lady as she looks up over the hillside toward Prescott and views large skeletons of ponderosa pines that could not outlive the drought.

The lower lawn also suffers in the dry heat. There is not enough water right now to keep growing things green. Hopefully the monsoon rains will stop their teasing and the heavy clouds will release much-needed moisture onto the parched ground.

Scotty, a Jerome resident for more years than most of us are old, tends to the garden around the Lady. Scotty loves the earth and growing things, and his patient hands are kind and gentle to the beleaguered plants and grass. The Lady admires his tender attention to the young grapevines planted along the rock walls. He mows the grass and makes sure that everything gets a good drink of water each day.

Scotty nurtures the young flowering plants, pulls weeds and makes sure that the watering system is working properly. He is a gem, and the Lady and I both appreciate him more than he knows.

Stories of old Jerome and its residents rattle around in his head, and he graciously shares them with me. Human interest tales of past times and people make for good listening, and Scotty knows all the secrets. Living in a small town is interesting, and although *you* may not always know what you are doing, everyone else in town does!

August carries the burden of increased humidity and sudden storms. Doors that opened easily just a few weeks ago now stick and often require a shoulder push to open. Windows are also sticky and hard to crank open. Evaporative cooling, very effective with low humidity, now pours more moisture into an already wet climate. Several monsoon storms move over a period of days into the Verde Valley. Cottonwood, just four miles down the hill, gets battered by a heavy dose of hail and intense rainfall. Jerome, on the other hand, receives but a few drops of the precious moisture.

The sky executes a most fascinating display of clouds. The storm flaunts a capricious show for those interested in watching as Mother Nature waves her arm and slides colors around like paint on a slippery canvas. Heavy black skies lighten to gray as rain pounds down upon the valley. The gray soon gives way to reds and golds as the sun beams through the clouds, contributing shafts of bright light. Dark clouds lighten as they spill their moisture toward the earth. Bright sunshine outlines fluffy white clouds drifting across the valley toward Cleopatra Hill. A last bit of moisture allows itself a slow trip to Jerome, and drenching rain finally blankets the town. The rain is so soft and so warm that every living thing – flowers, trees and even humans – reaches upward to embrace the moisture. The next day, plants that were stooped over and wilted stand straight and tall, having absorbed the life-giving rain. Although the rain was much needed, complaints abound later about the resulting humidity. The Lady just nods her head and smiles at these complaints. She welcomes the rain for her petticoat, which is trimmed with colorful flowers.

After weeks of seemingly problem-free sprinkling, now that the timers are all in and working, some of the sprinkler heads begin cracking and shattering. Again, and this time with Scotty standing only four feet away, the ground shudders, and a large section of the dry stack wall gives a sigh and slides and tumbles to the level below. At the apex of the 12-foot wall, near an area that Harry and I had some concern about, the boulders fall. There had been talk of constructing a stairway to the lower levels. Thinking the big old wall would hold, and in the interest of time, we moved on, leaving the wall alone. Funny how problems have a way of returning whether or not you invite them. I meet with Harry, and we decide that this might be a good time to build the stairway. Work will start in about two weeks, and in the meantime, Scotty shuts off the sprinklers to that area to prevent any further damage to the walls.

Because the Lady is at the end of the line, water pressure at the Honeymoon Cottage varies from 25 PSI to over 180 PSI. This variance wreaks havoc on the sprinkler heads, at times blowing them apart as the pressure literally makes the pipes sing and stresses the system. Water is gravity fed to town from the mountains and has a mind of its own at times. The next Friday, Mark Wilcox, the plumber, will install a 2-foot regulator and a pop-off valve to bring some stability to the watering system.

Jack Davis, a talented stone setter from Camp Verde, will begin to lay the slate in the Little House on Saturday. Having felt neglected for so long, the Little House eagerly awaits redressing. All three-and-a-half bays will be tiled and decorated. The bride's room will boast a triptych mirror, where one can see themselves from all sides, and preparation stations for attendants. Upstairs in the honeymoon suite, decorating will begin. Together, the Lady and the Little House smile at what the future holds.

Up in town, I volunteer at the Chamber of Commerce Visitor Center. The old horse-drawn carriage often parks next to the Chamber and offers rides around town. Bob has had great success with his small town tour. With about a million-and-a-half tourists a year passing through Jerome, there are ample customers who want to sit on the old leather seats in the "surrey with the fringe on top" and bounce around the old streets.

All Good Things Must Come to an End

*B*rown wild wheat sways to and fro as the afternoon wind gently teases its dry stalks. Wildflowers scatter seeds into the air as they come to the end of their life cycle. All the greenery is drying now as the days become shorter and the cool nights become longer. Fall has arrived, silently creeping up on all of us with no warning other than a drop in temperature in the mornings and evenings. Shorter days signal to all growing things that it is time to cast their progeny to the winds to guarantee a continuance of life in the next year.

Spiders are moving into the house, and a large wolf spider hangs on his web as if suspended in the air above the kitchen sink window. On an early morning, I walk into a string of sticky web spun to trap an unsuspecting moth. Mother Nature is sending out secret signals to her children that winter is quickly approaching. Indian summer peeks out from behind a pine tree, awaiting his opportunity to dance by the light of the full moon. When Jack Frost nips his toes, he, too, will retreat to wait out the ensuing winter. All around Jerome, the paradise trees hang heavy with blossoms, now dry and brown. The roses that line the upper rock wall are profuse with buds that open every morning to greet the sunshine, wishing for every stalk to enjoy one last blossom. Dark green leaves and thick stems affirm acceptance of their location. Within a month or so, they will be cut back to sleep out the winter. On the front lawn, yellow leaves now litter the grass as the apricot tree prepares for winter. Being one of the earliest to leaf out, it is also one of the first to expose bare limbs. The apple, peach and plum trees will soon follow suit.

The Lady welcomes an open window in the early afternoon, and curtains wave as the wind moving through the canyons enters the house through the guest room and exits from the breakfast room. A small bird flies in through an open window, and both dogs give chase. Puzzled at this feathery flying object that alights on the curtain rod, they both sit and stare. Eventually, the little bird flies down the stairway to the basement and out an open window. Outside, elegant monarch butterflies kiss the purple flowers of the butterfly plants and sit for but a moment on the red and yellow lantanas before they glide off to mate, lay their eggs and then give up their short-lived lives. There isn't much left of their energy after a lengthy flight from Brazil.

Soft yellow paint now dresses the Lady, and her blue roof complements her genteel look. Small pink oleanders border her front window. "Bright eyes" (vincas) bloom profusely between the oleanders. Iris rhizomes, planted just a few weeks ago after being rescued from a flowerbed by the winery, have sent strong straight leaves up through the ground. The irises will not bloom until next spring, so they are sharing the flowerbed with moss roses that are a riot of color. During the past few months, all the flowers and shrubs have established a good root base and now provide us with a full spectrum of color in all directions. "Everything is so lovely," the Lady thinks. She feels so very beautiful, and rightly so. Along the edge of the first terrace rock wall, rose bushes, rosemary, blue hibiscus, African daises and bright red and pink petunias provide a rainbow of color. They also provide a barrier for the curious who might be tempted to get too close to the edge. The 12-foot drop would make for a quick trip to the next terrace…or the emergency room.

The Lady turns and smiles at the Little House that sits proudly beside her. The Bridal Salon is completed. A triptych mirror, attendant stations, black slate flooring, new near-white carpet upstairs in the honeymoon suite, with a new four-poster bed and dresser to match, please both of them. The Lady loves the finery and the flowered custom bedspread, pillows and curtains.

The large pine trees in the garden party area just south of the Little House have survived the bark beetle plague due to lots and lots of water and loving care from Scotty. The needles that were brown and dropping are now replaced with green needles, and new growth appears at the tips of all the branches. A copper bird feeder attracts many kinds of birds that chirp and twitter all day long as each species comes to feed. Some eat from the feeder tray, and others are ground feeders. There is enough seed for all, the Little House thinks, as the birds fuss and feud, each one of them greedier than the next.

On October 11, the Lady and I will host our many friends and workers who saw the vision, felt the passion and brought us to where we are today. A cookout, a ride on the horse-drawn carriage, a local band and fun and companionship are planned. What a journey these last two years have been.

It all began in August 2001, as a friend and I walked around a broken and bent-over structure. Parts of the journey were frightening and some were even painful, but the overall experience was downright pleasurable. A few final touches, like copper rain gutters, are yet to be installed; tulip bulbs are to be planted in mulched flowerbeds to await the spring thaw, but most of the renovation is complete.

Each visitor to Jerome who glances to their right as they make the turn by the old high school on their way up to town sees the Lady and the Little House. As historic landmarks they proudly share their legacy. The Lady sits atop five terraced walls facing the future with calm and grace. She holds a title she has earned. Love made all the difference, as she again reigns as the Jewel of Jerome.

Epilogue

$\mathcal{I}$t seems like it is all over just as it is all beginning, but the end is here. Love and care will keep the Lady and the Little House in good condition as I enjoy and share the fruits of the past two years' labor. Sitting on the swing overlooking the setting sun or enjoying a cup of coffee in the morning as the sun rises, I delight in the company of the Lady. And the story ends with this chapter, I move into a new chapter of life with my children.

The Jerome Winery opened to raving crowds on September 19, 2003. Weddings and parties at the Lady have been planned. On October 24, the Jerome Historical Society hosts the first ever Ghost Walk. Visitors will have the opportunity to speak with Jerome residents playing the part of historical leaders. Peggy Douglas, the first mistress of the Lady, will be portrayed by me. "Pete" Douglas, the son of Lewis and Peggy, tells me about his mother as we speak on the phone. How coincidental that I am so like her. Does life repeat itself? Or is this just the circle that goes round and round and consummates where it all began? The Lady turns her head and looks over her shoulder. She winks and smiles knowingly as she walks into the future.

Update: Where We Are Today – December 2008

The Lady walks slowly around her yard enjoying the fragrant blooming flowers. She glances at the fruit trees and remembers when they were but thin sticks with nary a leaf. Today they are full of fruit, tall and healthy and will be pleased to release their bounty again next spring. The grass is lush and green and begs for mowing on a regular basis.

The Little House has been a delight to the Lady, whose maternal instincts took over when the little place was completed. The honeymoon suite is enjoyed by family and guests often, and when the bridal suite was dismantled, another guest room developed. At one time the Lady and I thought we would host weddings and special events. After several weddings and parties, however, the quiet and serenity of the home were lost. Both myself and the Lady longed for the peace and quiet we both enjoy so much to return, so it was a mutual decision to keep ourselves to ourselves once again.

The iron maiden has aged well nestled close to the house and plays host to many flowers planted in wine barrel halves, creating a colorful border all around her. How pleasing, she thinks, that I live in the middle of a sunny flower garden after spending so many years in the dark hull of a ship moving back and forth across the ocean. She keeps all her garden tools neat and tidy, the ladders and wheelbarrows orderly.

Unfortunately, the wonderful wedding of Jason and Carrie ended in divorce. These two people with two very different perspectives had a difficult time making their marriage work. Sometimes circumstances intervene and, for a myriad of reasons, it just doesn't last. The Lady is sad that the first union made on her grounds did not endure. However, an active, bright 3½-year-old girl now delights all with her smile as she runs across the yard with Lucky. This past year, Copper went to heaven. She slept in the shade of the Lady on the lawn in the summer and curled up next to the radiators in the winter. We all miss her very much. Lucky still carries his play toys, one at a time, out to the lawn in the hopes that Copper will pick one up so he can give chase.

Every October the Lady hosts the Jerome Humane Society Benefit Brunch on the front lawn. Rosemary hedges now frame the yard like a wide green ribbon. Guests enjoy wonderful food prepared by Marge Mitchell, Erin Ryan, San Francisco gourmet chef; Lou Currier, long time resident and our own Jerome resident gourmet chef, and other volunteers. Sally Dryer and Patrick Lincoln tend bar, serving Mimosas, Bloody Marys and, this year, sparkling peach wine from the Jerome Winery. Everyone has a wonderful time promoting a very good cause. The quilt show that follows the brunch is a delight and wonder to behold. Each year, four or five quilters use the same colors, fabric and theme, yet each one produces a unique quilt. The talents of these many varied quilters remind us of the individuality and creativity that abounds in this small mountain town. There is an auction and a lot of money is raised to help Jerome animals and keep the clinic open. The Lady is always pleased to host the brunch. She eavesdrops on the many conversations and tries to catch up with everyone's busy lives. She finds the auction very exciting as the bidding goes up higher and higher. Lee Hay Martin, of Designs on You, made a very unique quilt this year, especially for the Jerome Humane Society; it has an animal design. The quilt brought a pretty penny to the Humane Society. The lucky bidder then graciously donated the quilt back to the Humane Society to hang on the wall in the clinic. Generosity is definitely not lacking in Jerome.

Most of her days are quiet as she and I grow old together. I enjoy the comfortable atmosphere with all the flowers and fruit trees as much as she does. We sit for long periods of time gazing across the yard over the rosemary hedge overlooking the Verde Valley. We enjoy the many cloud formations that change minute by minute. We can see all the way to Sedona's red rocks. Storms are most exciting with thunder and lightning putting on the best fireworks show we have ever seen.

The Jerome Winery quickly became a great success. The vineyard in Wilcox had its first harvest this year, and John and I hand-pressed 400 gallons of grapes to make into wine. The Lady laughed as I held up hands stained purple from the skin of the grapes. In a couple of years we will see how successful our wine-making efforts were. All the residue of pressed grapes was spread around the bottoms of the trees and into flowerbeds so the organic enzymes and vitamins would go back into the earth. Unfortunately, flies thought this was a great place to lay their eggs. The Lady was swishing away these unwanted guests for weeks, and I was severely admonished despite my good intentions.

I have made many friends in this small town, many of whom are members of the Jerome Volunteer Humane Society. I helped furnish a new clinic in the old bomb shelter at the Clark Street Elementary School, which is also now home to the offices of the mayor and town council. The building houses the Jerome Public Library that offers many services to the community, such as videos, free computer use, educational classes and extremely well-stocked bookshelves. In this old building, Jerome conducts business and serves its citizens.

I often walk up to town from the Honeymoon Cottage to visit the post office and pick up my mail. The Jerome Post Office is an old relic of the past. Everyone in town goes to the post office to pick up their mail from wooden combination lock boxes. Items of interest are posted on the bulletin board in the lobby and make for good reading some days.

Thousands of tourists flock to Jerome, drawn by the allure of the "Wickedest Town in the West"; the "Largest Ghost Town in America"; the annual Historic Home Tour; the Garden Tour; Ghost Walk weekend; and many other events and reasons. The crooked streets and the interesting history of what once was must be hard-wired into our genes. With our modern lives so sophisticated, complicated and fast-paced, visitors to Jerome see a simpler, slower way of life and a peek into the past. We who live in Jerome revel in the many rumors about our ghostly inhabitants and their antics. There are many stories about ghost sightings and events caused by prior residents. Most will say, "They are just having a good time." This is what Jerome is all about – having a good time and looking into our history.

As I walk back to the Honeymoon Cottage, down sloping, cracked and broken sidewalks, I see damage from years ago. Many buildings are marred, and some were totally destroyed by dynamite blasting from the mines' 87 miles of tunnels beneath town. Walking toward the house along Douglas Road, I pass the old Little Daisy iron elevators (called A-frames) that once carried miners into the mines. I turn and walk down Bell Road toward the Honeymoon Cot-